If you are wondering whether to share your mistakes and pain, if you think your past is too ugly for God, think no more. Kasey walks us through the hardest parts of *our* story by letting us see *her* ugly turned lovely. *Nothing Wasted* is raw, ugly, beautiful, horrifying, sad, and exhilarating. My world is better because I read this book.

—MISSY ROBERTSON, *DUCK DYNASTY*; FOUNDER, LAMININ AND THE MIA MOO FUND

Kasey writes from a place of honesty and brokenness. If you wonder whether God can use someone like you, read this book! God brings beauty from ashes, every time we let him.

—KAREN KINGSBURY, NOVELIST, *TWO WEEKS*

A deeply encouraging message of hope and grace that no matter the brokenness or pain, God, in his love, is in the midst of it and is always at work to redeem and bring forth new life.

—TIM AND JULIE CLINTON

Kasey articulately and convincingly helps us realize that God takes every part of our stories and uses them in ways we never could have imagined. Her words are like reading a letter from a dear friend. She will make you think, cry, and laugh, and point you to a God who loves us and offers redemption at every twist and turn life takes.

—MELANIE SHANKLE, AUTHOR AND SPEAKER

Kasey's love for God is evident as she brings you on her journey. This book will encourage and challenge you to trust him with more than the pretty parts of your story. When it feels like everything is going wrong, remember that God says *nothing* is wasted.

—JADA EDWARDS, WOMEN'S PASTOR; AUTHOR, *THE CAPTIVE MIND*

This book is an offering to Jesus. In it Kasey washes his feet with her tears and dries them with her hair and anoints them with oil, because she is compelled to express her love for the one who can't not love her. If you are willing to see yourself in Kasey and Justin's story, your heart will be inspired to love him like crazy too.

—Dr. Dan Marshall (Kasey and Justin's
pastor), senior pastor, Faith Bible Church

Simply powerful! Out of the ashes of all of our brokenness there is always forgiveness, reconciliation, healing, and redemption. You want to get closer to God? Read this book. Then open your heart to your own brokenness so you too can be redeemed.

—Alan Graham, founder/CEO, Mobile Loaves
and Fishes; author, Welcome Home(less)

I know firsthand what it feels like to have a life that feels too wrong to be rescued, too broken to be healed. But I also know what it feels like to watch God do the impossible with it. Nothing is wasted, friend. If you need a word to help you hold on to that truth, Kasey Van Norman and her story are exactly what you need.

—Michele Cushatt, author, Relentless

Forgiving Kasey was the most difficult thing I've ever had to do, yet in those dark days, the Holy Spirit called to my heart, "To God be the glory!" As crazy as it sounds, I would not change a single piece of our story. Kasey transparently shares the good, the bad, and the ugly parts of our lives, including poor decisions, infidelity, forgiveness, and a cancer diagnosis. Trusting God in these heartwrenching moments has been difficult. It's hard to believe that people will actually read the intimate and vulnerable parts of our story, but how could we not share what God has done with and through us? I can truly say, no part of our story has been wasted. Thank you for letting us share it with you.

—Justin Van Norman, Kasey's husband

NOTHING WASTED

NOTHING
WASTED

GOD USES THE STUFF YOU WOULDN'T

KASEY VAN NORMAN

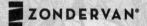

ZONDERVAN®

ZONDERVAN

Nothing Wasted
Copyright © 2019 by Kasey Van Norman

Requests for information should be addressed to:
Zondervan, *3900 Sparks Dr. SE, Grand Rapids, Michigan 49546*

Zondervan titles may be purchased in bulk for educational, business, fundraising, or promotional use. For information, please email SpecialMarkets@Zondervan.com.

ISBN 978-0-310-35716-2 (softcover)

ISBN 978-0-310-35733-9 (audio)

ISBN 978-0-310-35731-5 (ebook)

Published in association with literary agent Jenni Burke of D.C. Jacobson & Associates LLC, an Author Management Company. www.dcjacobson.com.

Cover design: Curt Diepenhorst
Cover illustration: iMacron / Shutterstock
Author photo: Philip Winham / @philipwinhamphoto
Interior design: Denise Froehlich

Printed in the United States of America

HB 03.09.2020

For those who think they're
too boring or too broken

Contents

Acknowledgments 11

1. When God Doesn't Stop It from Happening 13
2. Running Naked through the Streets of Your Story . . 27
3. Starched Shirts and Supernatural Sightings 37
4. Too Tired to Fight 49
5. Attach: Did You or Didn't You? 65
6. Parental Predisposition Problems 75
7. Dusting Off Daddy Issues 83
8. Feeling Our Way to God 93
9. Let's Talk about Sex . . . or Not 103
10. Life-Defining Moments 117
11. Honesty's a Buzz Kill 127
12. Listening to the Right Voice 135
13. It's All Just One, Big Setup 143
14. When Nothing and Everything Changes 155
15. Sift It Out Now, Sinner 165
16. I Don't Know How to Not Love You 181
17. Living Like It's Our Job 195
18. Big-Picture Believing: A Home for Unlikely,
    Improbable, and Discarded Things 205

Notes 219

Acknowledgments

THE FOLLOWING NAMES SHOULD BE ON THE FRONT COVER:

Justin, thank you for loving me so irrationally and supernaturally that people will want to read about it. Thank you for loving Jesus more than me. Your confidence in Christ gives me permission to put this book out there. I adore you for living your whole life in the light. And fighting for me to do the same. I love you so much.

Emma Grace and Lake, you know most of this story, but not all of it. I'd be nervous if it weren't for the rock-solid Spirit God has given each of you to see and discern well beyond your years. Thank you for being two of my greatest champions. Every day I get to "mama" you is another day I get to do what I was born to do. I love you so much.

Tracy Singleton, I am calling you out because you're the friend who has never, ever given up on me. Thank you for standing by my side, even when I'm wrong. Thank you for modeling the sweet spot of grace and justice where I want to live, and for teaching me so many of the lessons I write about here. I love you.

Jamie Schneringer, I am calling you out because you're the friend who helps me believe in who I want to be, the friend who chose me when others didn't. Your unrelenting affirmation and loyalty to my heart has gotten me through the many years and tears it's taken me to write this book. Thank you. I love you.

Thank you to my **Faith Bible Church Bryan** family. I didn't believe that church could really feel like family. You proved me wrong. I love you for it.

Jenni Burke, thank you for being the literary agent of my dreams, but also and mainly a really good friend. You're the peanut butter to my jelly. You get my heart and you see it through the fog of first drafts and chaotic visionary rants. I love you.

Carolyn McCready and Sara Riemersma, thank you for taking a risk on a gal like me. You make the big world of publishing feel just a bit smaller. From a postconference callback to calm my nerves, to a tearful shoulder shake reminding me that God has gone before, I am deeply grateful that I get to have you both as cheerleaders and friends.

Margot Starbuck, Brian Phipps, and Kendall Davis, thank you for scrubbing this thing until it shined! So many words. I would have quit. So glad you didn't.

To **Alicia, Robin, Beth, Alyssa**, and the entire **Harper Collins / Zondervan** team who have served and will continue to serve this message through countless hours of fine-tuning, I thank you.

To the cool kids at **52 Watt Studio**. Thank you for creating over-the-top video for this project. I don't even know how that happened, considering the "farm noise" and "roadkill" incidents. You're the Harry Potters of video curriculum.

Thank you, **Philip Winham**, for being young and way more right-brained than me. Who would have thought a wall and random room under construction would lend headshots I don't hate. Don't stop taking pictures. You're really good.

CHAPTER 1

When God Doesn't Stop It from Happening

"Kasey," his voice raspy and solemn from hours of crying, "we knew this day would come."

His voice was as familiar to me as the lines on my face. I had never spent more time on the phone with a man, not even my husband. Tone, inflection, silence, number of breaths between thoughts—all of it had become an art to us, the only thing we could create and give meaning to together.

"She knows. This is the last time . . ." He didn't need to finish the sentence.

As his words choked short, I gasped and let the tension hang for what I knew would be our final seconds together. Then without another word, we hung up.

Click. Dial tone.

STORM'S A BREWIN'

The day we knew would come was the farthest thing from the minds of four, doe-eyed newlyweds meeting for the first time in our church's young marrieds Sunday school class. Justin and I loved Ty and Rachel from the moment we hesitantly slid our metal folding chairs next to theirs under the unflattering, florescent lights. Our first greeting to one another echoed through the church gym, especially Justin's. I was beginning to wonder if my new husband had spoken in anything close to a whisper a day in his life. Without one ounce of insecurity, hesitation, or discretion, Justin bellowed in a loud, southern drawl like a Texas Republican running for office, "Howdy! How y'all doin'?!" thrusting his hand toward Ty's chest. I flashed an awkward smile toward Rachel with a shade of embarrassment. To my surprise, she returned my look with a small nod and half smile of her own. Her eyes grew wide with an "I get you girl" expression as Ty replied at a matching decibel level.

"I'm Ty! This is my wife, Rachel. Y'all join us!"

Rachel and I chuckled under our breath to one another. She already felt like someone I'd known forever. *Please be my friend*, I telepathically thought, middle-school Kasey stepping to the front of my brain. Thank God Rachel's preteen insecurities waved back.

From that moment on, she and I were inseparable.

The four of us were instant friends, thrilled to find a couple who might help us cross that strange wasteland from single to married, where old friends drop like flies and new friends lie scarce on the horizon.

Barely twenty-two years old and packing college degrees with nowhere to point them, the four of us were riding the wave of passion and naivety, Rachel and I still able to turn our spouses' disgusting oddities, like chewing a three-month-old toothpick kept in the sweaty brim of a cap, into endearing attributes.

We were free spirits. Friends who felt like home. Laughing until our sides split from our first failed attempt to fry chicken, which resulted in repainting her entire kitchen, lamenting late into the night over impossible dreams and the arduous calling to "live on love." (We were broke.) Then jumping up and down scream-sobbing when Rachel's and my pregnancy tests showed positive within weeks of one another. Twice.

As years passed, the eight of us (two babies each) gained hometown celebrity status as the dream team of "Christian community." Justin and Ty, now business professionals, were successful at work and sought-after mentors at church, both men of integrity, doting fathers, and devoted husbands. Rachel and I could be found any day of the week hosting supper club, teaching Bible study, rehearsing with the church choir, or decorating the fellowship hall for a wedding shower, all while sipping a latte with one hand and burping a baby with the other.

To onlookers, we were #bestfriendgoals. But to us, we were family—experiencing the same firsts together, caring for each other, entrusting one another with vulnerabilities we dared not show in public.

Rachel and I were inseparable. Together, we picked out carpet for our living rooms, then took a nap on that carpet the first day our kids were finally old enough to attend preschool. We grabbed one another's same-size jeans from the pile of dirty laundry on the floor because somebody pooped on our clean ones (children not always being the culprit).

Our ability to purchase a home, return to prebaby weight, and color-coordinate monograms had the new herd of younger newly-weds at church clamoring around us. "How do you do it?" they asked. "Teach us your ways!" they teased. "No, really."

So when the tenured leaders of our Sunday school class decided to step down, we felt called to step up. I mean, who better to lead thirty-six couples through the biblical foundations of covenant marriage than two families responsible for their first mortgages, raising pairs of toddlers, and seasoned with invaluable experience, the oldest of us twenty-six?

God can restrain the wind and the rain with just a word (Luke 8:24–25), command the dead to live again (John 11:43–44), and uphold the entire universe with his power (Heb. 1:3). But he did not stop this day from happening. Foreseeing the future, ordering and unfolding the events of humanity in accordance with his will, God allowed Justin and Kasey to meet Ty and Rachel, grow to love them, cherish them, and be known intimately by them.

All the while, and unbeknownst to us, a tsunami gained strength miles from the coast of this blissful, serene friendship. A tiny earthquake, undetectable to human senses, rumbled beneath our naive feet. And God, sovereignly able to call it off or at the very least to yell, "Run for your lives!" had no intention of stopping it.

THE BEGINNING OF THE END

I think all of our life-altering ends find their beginning in the same four words Satan posed as a question to Eve in the garden: "Did God really say?"

"Kasey, did God *really* say he doesn't need your help running the universe?"

"Did God really say you are enough right where you are?"

"Kasey, did God really say Justin is the right guy for you—forever? What if Justin really knew you—who you've been, what you've done? Would he stay then, love you then?"

"Did God *really* say you must not eat from just *any* tree in the garden?"

No wonder Paul compared the Christians of Corinth to Eve's worst day when he confessed how scared he was for them. Paul was afraid that just like Eve, they would be deceived by the serpent's cunning and their minds led astray from their sincere and pure devotion to Christ (2 Cor. 11:3). Even now, his warning echoes through the corridor of our twenty-first-century church that, just like our first mother, Eve, smack dab in the middle of everything she could possibly want or need, God's chosen can still be lured into believing it isn't enough. That even the most authentic and committed Christ-followers can find themselves beguiled by Satan's charms, blind to the truth and belly-up in painful repercussion.

Chances are good you have witnessed another's radical fall from spiritual high to sinful snare. You and I have both read the news feed of some megatalented evangelical leader blazing a trail of discipleship toward the mountaintop of godly zeal when out of nowhere they found themselves plummeting toward humility and humiliation from the slam of seduction they never saw coming.

Even the most compassionate among us can sit bewildered, saddened, or shocked by the fall of a righteous person. Isn't it strange how we can feel slightly offended, even though they are a stranger to us and we have no clue what really happened?

I think that spectator zing in us manifests our having convinced ourselves we would never do *that*. The truth is, the amount of pride it takes to conceive that thought is the precise amount it takes to stumble into our own sinful pitfall. Or at least to seriously consider Satan's question, "Did God really say?"

May we not forget that Satan's ultimate fight is with God. And because Satan knows he is not powerful enough to land an attack on his true nemesis, he will use all of his time and resources to wage war on the next best thing—God's real, authentic children.

The crash-and-burn kind of sin that rips apart families, friends, and church congregations is most often ignited by the hottest burning coal among them. Whoever in your group is the most willing to be authentic, the most devoted to their calling, the most passionate about serving others, the most committed to Bible reading, the one who is seemingly good at everything, the one you are quick to call for help and to model yourself after, they are the one with the largest target on their back.

Because Satan is in the business of high-profile temptation, his sights are set on those with the most integrity to lose. He wants to gather as many onlookers as possible under the banners of ministry, fellowship, and accountability. His goal is to make the cover of *Church People Magazine,* so he will toss in a temptation that speaks to the part of us he has studied the longest—our weakness. Capitalizing on our fear, shame, inadequacy, and wounding, he circles us like a lion, waiting for just the right amount of spiritual favor on our life before he pounces. He waits for our mountaintop moment, the time when we have gained just enough confidence to finally and wholeheartedly step into leadership, teaching, parenting, advocating, calling (1 Peter 5:8).

Suddenly we have people watching us, and we have limited time to adjust to the new and ever-changing expectations of us. People like us, follow us, listen to us, develop an opinion about us based on the filtered frame of social media.

Most onlookers' understanding of us is just limited enough to make it easy for them to walk away, unfollow, or unfriend whenever we fall.

In my own nosedive down the mountain, I was shocked by how quickly I felt overtaken by the urge to distrust God after years on the straight and narrow. I was even more surprised by how few friends were waiting at the bottom to catch me or at the very least to throw me a bandaid Bible verse or two.

One minute, I was on a high of living my best life now! I had it all—the good ol' boy husband who would take a bullet for me, healthy children, my dream home nestled in the heart of East Texas complete with white picket fence and a kitchen overflowing with friends on any given night. I had a good reputation in my thirty-thousand-member hometown (no small feat) and the respect of my church as a leader, both as a woman and as a *young* woman (again, no small feat in the Southern Baptist, white evangelical, Bible Belt of the world).

Then in the very next minute, all of it came crashing to the ground with the sound of a dial tone.

After months of dismissing her gut instinct, Rachel decided to dig deeper into our phone records. Her search through old texts and calls surfaced the one thing none of us ever thought would be possible that day we met in the gym.

Like Eve, my intention was never to distrust God. Like her, I loved God, knew him and spent daily time with him. It was unlikely I would turn my back on him over something as simple as attraction to the wrong man. Like Eve, I had to think about my decision, spend time turning the fruit over and over in my hands—smell it, position it on the mantel so I could stand back and stare at it a few weeks before biting into it.

Also, like Eve, I did something much more devastating than just take a bite of fruit; I used my love for God to justify disobeying him. Over time, I convinced myself that God needed my help. Help running my marriage, my friendships, my life.

The longer I pondered Satan's question, the more reasonable it became. Maybe I did understand parts of Ty that Rachel didn't. Perhaps Ty did need my emotional support if their marriage was to be successful. Maybe Justin really wouldn't care that I sneaked out of bed each night to "counsel" Ty over the phone, it being ministry, accountability, community, and all. If the fruit helped our marriages be wise and more like God, why wouldn't I eat it?

Had you cornered me under those florescent lights and told me that a devoted Christian like myself would plunge headlong into the valley of a three-year affair with her best friend's husband, I would have laughed arrogantly in your face.

As it turned out, I did indeed laugh. Just not from the top of a mountain.

BUSTED-BELLY LAUGH

In those moments after hearing Ty's voice for the last time, alone in my house in the silence of napping children and surrounded by five loads of unfolded clothes, the next sound I heard caught me off guard in every way.

Laughter. My own.

And not just tiny, breathless sighs or a chuckle but hysterical, from the belly, loud enough to wake my kids and throw my feet scissor-kicking in the air kind of laughter.

It sounds horrible, I know. Here I am holding a ticking time bomb that will destroy everyone around me and I'm *laughing*.

Had anyone else been in the room, I would have felt embarrassed or guilty. But as years of shackles fell to the ground and the weight of secrecy lifted from my shoulders, my heart erupted in such pure freedom that it could not help but spill over with laughter.

Rachel knew the truth. Ty said it was over. Maybe I could finally be free.

The courage to confess that I'd begged and pleaded for was suddenly forced upon me. I was no longer in control, no longer blind or deceived. My mind was more awake and clear than it had been in years. The lie I'd worked my entire life to preserve was laid bare and broken at the foot of the mountain.

I had no idea what life would be like one hour, one week, or one year from this moment. My mind raced in a million directions. Would Justin leave, take our kids, what was Rachel thinking, would she take their kids, who would we, the crushed dream team, become?

All I knew was that life would never be the same. Out of sincere gratitude for that fact, I laughed.

Maybe life could finally make sense now that I wasn't running it. Now that plates were no longer spinning above my head, I could finally take a good, hard look through all of the broken pieces on the floor.

The lie I pampered and put makeup on and played with in secret could be seen for what it was—fear. Fear I would never be enough, fear no one could love the most honest version of me, fear that I, a devoted church girl, was capable of scandalous, horrible things just like the next girl. Fear that I was exactly who I thought I was—needy.

Maybe fear is the one who talks us into climbing the mountain of self-reliance in the first place. Even at the beginning, no ordinary temptation or feeling would have been strong enough to convince Adam and Eve to turn on their Father after all those years of peace, provision, and pleasure. It would have to be the one thing designed to be given only to God, and therefore, utterly destructive when given to man. The line easily blurred or distorted in the human heart, which is made always to be worshiping something.

Most people think that fear is a lack of faith. But it takes great faith to fear. Faith is hoping in something we cannot see. Fear functions in a similar way. When we are scared, it

> **Fear is not lack of faith. Fear is questioning God's love for us.**

is easy to have faith in the "what if" scenarios we make up in our heads but are not necessarily true. At its core, fear is not lack of faith. Fear is questioning God's love for us.

How clever, Satan. We call your bluff. Use God to turn us against him. Distract us just long enough to switch the awe-inspiring fear of God into the pride-inducing fear of man. Use the cloak of godliness to disguise the subtle shift from "God is enough" to "I'm not enough."

Which leads me back to what God really said.

FREEDOM TREE

God really did command Adam and Eve not to eat from the tree of the knowledge of good and evil and warn them that to do so would bring death. But what Eve seemed to forget in her conversation with the serpent was what else God really said. "You are free. Free to eat anything and everything else. Free to create, work, have sex. Free to rest in the life-sustaining peace that because I am God, you don't have to be." (See Gen. 2:15–17.)

I think this is why God put the tree in the middle of the garden in the first place, there to remind us we are not meant to know everything, not designed to rule the universe or single-handedly give meaning to the world around us. We are not capable of rescuing, healing, or saving people. Instead, we have been given miles and miles of provision with one, loving promise—we are free not to be God.

On that dark, terrible afternoon of March 9, 2009, I laughed because life as I knew it was over. Death had finally come to the fear-made gods within me: perfection and punishment.

The perfect house, reputation, church work, and doting husband, all a ploy to keep myself and others distracted from the dark and twisty parts of me. The adultery, and every toxic, corrupt behavior leading up to it, was a way to punish myself for my past. My desires for perfection and punishment were conceived in fear and fed on shame and grew in the pride of believing that God needed my help.

The next time we want to dig our heels into the side of a pride mountain for the sake of perfection or out of fear of punishment, may we not forget he really did say.

God really did say that he alone is the measure of all that is true, good, and right in this world. He placed a tree in the middle of our lives to remind us of our mortality and his sovereignty over those attributes. He knew how devastated we would be when our version of truth, goodness, and justice proved to be ever-changing, misunderstood, and packed with impossibly high standards.

So we remember our freedom tree, the tree of God's sovereignty, his full command over all created beings. We remember it each time we fail, disappoint, wound, suffer, feel rejected, and can't fix it. We slam into it the moment we realize that even on our best days, we are still in need of saving.

> God really did say he alone is the measure of all that is true, good, and right in this world.

Just as he did for Adam and Eve, he is doing for us even now. He walks and talks with us, moves toward not away from us, and calls us out of hiding. He does this through all of our relationships and experiences, in every degree of feeling on the human spectrum. God is using our stories to reveal himself to us. He is the "author of our faith" (Heb. 12:2) and constantly working in our lives to make all things new (Rev. 21:5).

He wants us to connect our minds to our bodies and our bodies to his Spirit. He wants our personalities to take on his personality as harmoniously and perfectly as possible this side of heaven so that we are left with zero doubt how intricately we are tied to him.

The problem is humans insist on remaking God in our own image instead of embracing the image we are created in—God's. So he places trees in our path all along life's journey. Trees of pain, loss, offense, sinfulness, and rebellion. All there to remind us that he's got this. Really.

Every fall down the mountain, from Adam and Eve's bite of fruit to our own tampering with the forbidden, begins with our desire to be God rather than enjoy what has already been given to us in God. Consequently, any effort to fix ourselves, others, or the universe according to our version of truth results only in further separation from God's truth.

Like Adam and Eve, we've been given this one life, our one story, to know and understand God's grand, eternal purpose—the best story.

So it's not enough to say that God uses our lives if he does not also design them.

What God permits, he permits for a reason. And that reason is his design.

If God foresees cells mutating into malignant tumors, tremors developing a tsunami that will wipe out a village, a young Christian wife walking dangerously close to the edge of an affair, and he doesn't stop it, what are we to say? When Satan and his demons are permitted to wreak havoc on this earth, bringing ruin to many, what are we to do? When an innocent, perfect son begs his father to rescue him from a horrific, terrible death that he does not deserve, and yet his Father does not stop it from happening, where are we to turn (Matt. 26:39)?

> **It's not enough to say that God uses our lives if he does not also design them.**

Although we are afflicted in every way, we are not crushed. Perhaps we are perplexed, but not driven to despair; persecuted, but not forsaken; struck down, but not destroyed. We hold on to the treasure within us—the tree of freedom, reminding us that the surpassing power belongs to God and not us (2 Cor. 4:7–9).

We never reduce the depths of riches and wisdom and knowledge of God and his unsearchable judgments and inscrutable ways (Rom. 11:33) to random evil or meaningless events.

We do not dare call God evil or sinful in his governing of the universe, because "his work is perfect, for all his ways are justice." He is a "God of faithfulness and without iniquity, just and upright is he" (Deut. 32:4).

How could I not laugh at the closets full of fig leaves I had stitched together over the years? Even on my best days, those handmade garments never covered the shame, fear, and rejection I felt inside.

I tried every high the world offers, used every religious tool in my "Biblebelt." I was a good person, memorized Scripture, served the needy, prayed, went to church. And yet here I was, stretched across my newly stained concrete floor in my perfectly decorated, thirty-five-hundred-square-foot home at the end of my self and still in need of saving.

My busted-belly laugh could be felt through the ages by all who came face to face with their darkest day and lived to tell the tale. I write this book for anyone who's at the end of themselves—bewildered, exhausted, trapped, ticked off, or just plain wrong. I write this book for all who are silently screaming, *Why, God?! How could you still love me? What in the world could you possibly want with a wreck like me?*

Because he didn't stop it—for me, for you, and for millions of people throughout history—he has a purpose for it. And if we don't believe our lives are designed and purposed by God, we will waste them.

This is our story—the beginning of our end, when God takes his rightful place as the greatest love of our lives. This is the moment we finally take him up on his offer to be exactly who he says he is.

> God doesn't waste our lives. He designs them on purpose, for purpose.

CHAPTER 2

Running Naked through the Streets of Your Story

An unimaginable thing happened to me in 2010. I was asked to write my story down on paper, in a book, for strangers to read, marking it forever in time. No delete button.

When *Named by God* released in 2012, I was a walking panic attack. Because I had just handed over my first draft for people to judge, love, hate, or give to their kids as a coloring book.

My comfort level with reflection was still in its infancy. My ability to be honest with others and myself about the tender places of my past was still finding its legs—stumbling around, falling into things, leaving a trail of drool everywhere it went. My heart had been calloused to grief and shame so long I was still unsure how my memories felt and what they meant for my future.

Yet here I was, with thirty whole years of credible experience, writing a book subtitled "Overcoming Your Past, Transforming Your Present, Embracing Your Future."

Just punch me in the face now. It's fine.

Regardless of how my mind has changed since then or how far removed I feel from that earlier version of myself, one thing can be said about my first book. It was honest.

Named by God was my first draft. And first drafts are always brutally, embarrassingly, awkwardly honest.

Our first drafts are our first attempts to organize the people and experiences in our past into present-day meaning. Drafts are reflections of our lives thus far, the process of attaching a *why* to what we believe about God, others, and ourselves.

As we think through the chapters of our lives that have been written, our minds dizzy. It's enough to make one ask, "How am I not dead?" or, "Have I been living at all?"

Remembering our first drafts is like running through the neighborhood with no clothes on and sober, coming face to face with the stories that have shaped who we are today—why we are guarded about *that*, why he left, why we shut down when she enters the room, and most painfully, why we've been wrong about some things all along.

SACRED SNAPSHOTS

As we remember our stories, snapshots of hurt that we've managed as mere records in memory push themselves to the front of our minds. Pictures of our past refuse to settle for being categorized, labeled, and filed away deep inside our souls to collect dust. Instead, they come forward in HD sound and color, forcing us to consider a wider, more fluid, and multidimensional account.

We line the walls of our homes and flood social media with endearing pictures of our childhoods, fun teenage shenanigans, our wedding days, college graduations, and laughing faces around warm meals or toasting our friends with a glass of wine. But there are other pictures. Pictures we don't store on our phones or show the public. A sacred collection of snapshots: the first time we felt rejected, the moral compromise we made never to feel rejected again, the embarrassing repercussions we live with even now because of it.

The more vulnerable, traumatizing, or embarrassing the snapshot, the deeper we tuck it away, disconnecting it from our identity as much as possible. It doesn't help that our self-care obsessed world constantly distracts us with comfort, with the often preached and repinned quote that "our past does not define us." I, too, am guilty of pounding these words from a podium and framing a watercolor rendition of them in my office. But the more I stare at them, the more annoyed and bewildered I become.

It's a well-intentioned statement, of course. Just not the most helpful.

I get what all of us broken believers are trying to say: God's opinion is the only one that matters. I may have done some stupid stuff in my past, but God sees me for who I really am. My identity is in Christ, not in the things I have done.

None of this is untrue. Take God up on his promise to save you through his Son, Jesus, and you betcha—you're new and clean and stand before him righteous, and his opinion *is* the only one that matters. Hallelujah. All the praise hands go here.

But as it often goes with hashtags, tweets, profile bios, and feel-good one-liners, there is oh so much more to the story.

> Behold, you delight in truth in the inward being,
>   and you teach me wisdom in the secret heart.
>
> Purge me with hyssop, and I shall be clean;
>   wash me, and I shall be whiter than snow.
> Let me hear joy and gladness;
>   let the bones that you have broken rejoice.
> —PSALM 51:6–8 ESV

Notice who gets the credit for the broken bones in this passage. Also notice what it takes to feel clean, washed, and whiter than snow after all of these bones have been broken—truth. And not just any truth, a purging truth, medicine for the most secret, sick places within us. That's what hyssop is, a medicinal plant used much like our modern-day antiseptic or expectorant, a small, aromatic bush from the mint family used mostly to open congested airways.

God wants us to breathe again! To know truth in our secret, sacred hearts, to open up the airways of our untouchable, unthinkable, unlovely, unlikely places.

Once we know his truth clearly in these tender, messy, congested parts of our story, we will indeed be joyful and glad to hear that all of the painful, embarrassing, horrific moments of our past have been given voices to celebrate the one who permitted them to break us in the first place. Only in the honesty of our stories will we feel purged and clean, washed and whiter than snow.

In light of this, I believe our past most certainly defines us. And that's a good thing.

I believe God has chosen us to know him not in spite of our past but through it. Why in the world would we not want to be defined by what he foresaw and predestined to be the very thing to conform us into his image (Rom. 8:29)?

After two decades of studying the brain, I can tell you that it's physiologically impossible to disconnect our identities from any person or experience in our past. We are all intricately tied to one another and deeply marked by our experiences, big and small.

God doesn't want to redefine our lives apart from our experiences, even the painful, shameful ones. Instead, he wants to tell us the truth about himself through others, our personalities, and the nonrandom sequence of events we call life.

I think that deep down we all believe, or at least want to believe, that this is true. Because regardless of how far away or forgotten a painful memory seems, we know it's still right there below the surface, silently shaping our thoughts and triggering our behaviors.

We may clean ourselves up, go to church, be nicer, more generous people. Maybe we don't drink or cuss as much as we used to. Maybe we give more money to charity or spend more time with our kids. But if we have not sorted through the sacred parts of our lives and recognized our most painful memories' purpose in shaping who we are becoming, those memories will fester and one day demand to be acknowledged, most often through an experience that is equally painful, if not more so. Without a healthy remembrance of the details of our past, we will repeat the pain in more socially acceptable ways.

When I submitted my very first manuscript to the publisher, I was fairly certain it was awesome. That was until I received the edits back only five days later. "Well, that was fast," I thought. "Guess it didn't need much work." Then I opened the file.

It looked as if a small squirrel had been mutilated on the pages—red lines crossing through whole sections, entire sentences deleted, and more than seventy-eight comments that said, "Reader doesn't know what you are saying"—all in chapter one.

My jaw hit the floor, tears streamed down my face, and a flood of unfiltered words broke loose from the most sinful place within me and forced my husband to shove our kids into the back yard.

I wanted to quit. Not just writing but life.

For days after, I refused to turn on my computer and instead binged old seasons of *Grey's Anatomy*. Irreverent thoughts ran through my mind. "How could she? Who does she think she is? Surely she hasn't lived enough life to be editing mine!"

But underneath my cheeky reactions lay the solid ground of truth—I was scared. And because I was so scared to tell the truth about my life, I had submitted a manuscript so polished and clean that it was obviously and embarrassingly inauthentic.

I didn't want to remember how confused and lost I'd felt as a child watching my parents fight, drink, and leave. I had no desire to relive the abuse and promiscuity of my teen years and the consequences that lingered shamefully long into my adulthood. Fresh from the exposure of my secret three-year adulterous relationship, I dared not press too firmly on that tender wound.

I knew I had struggled with depression, addiction, self-harm, and loads of insecurity, but somewhere along the way, I had disconnected from it all. I had pushed my most painful memories so deep within me that I had become blind to the truth that the story I was sharing with others, the one I was believing for myself, was not the real one.

The editor wanted my first draft, not some polished up, pretty version of the story I wished I'd lived. Not the filtered pieces reserved for Instagram. She wanted my guts on the floor—the vulnerable, hard, messy, sacred snapshots of my heart where I'd struggled, hurt, questioned, and been wrong about so many things.

She wanted the real story.

The true one.

TELL ME A STORY

I don't have to convince you that as a species, we are obsessed with story.

Not only are our lives equipped with all the great elements of story (setting, characters, protagonists and antagonists, conflict, tragedy, drama, mystery, adventure, romance), we also crave it.

This makes sense, right? It's why we read, watch movies, listen to music, talk to people, creep social media, play video games, write words, sing words—all the things!

Story has connected human beings throughout history as

both the oldest and most beloved form of communication and understanding. So we just keep on obsessing over it. As a culture, everything we create (or think about creating) revolves around how to tell a great story, a story that people will buy, invest in, spend money on, believe in, not walk away from.

And as we know, storytelling works.

From the 1400s to the 1700s, stories came to us in print. In the 1800s, we had the telegraph and the telephone. In the 1900s, stories were brought to life by radio, television, the computer, the internet, and mobile phones. And now, in the twenty-first century, we hold lifetimes of stories from around the globe in the palms of our hands. We are able to see and talk to others in real time, read books, watch movies, listen to music, anywhere we are, whenever we want, all with a few clicks of some buttons.

Jesus spent more time telling stories than he ever did preaching.

He knew what we also know, that our stories connect us to the parts of us that are the same—our ability to hurt or love and our insatiable search for meaning.

God, the master storyteller, created us to crave the arch of a storyline. So he wrote our stories to best connect us to his story.

Understanding his divine story gives meaning, hope, and direction to our lives. But we spend more time studying and questioning the lives and motivations of others on Facebook than we do studying and questioning our own lives and motivations.

We wrongly believe that the arch of our story is either too boring or too scandalous to be significant to God.

We wrongly believe that the arch of our story is either too boring or too scandalous to be significant to God.

While I am guilty of the latter, my friend Christina best explains the former.

During lunch one day, Christina confessed to me that because her home was safe, because she grew up in church with parents who loved her and never experienced a trauma to speak of, her life was boring and simple compared with others'.

Over the years, Christina sat through numerous testimonies in which women shared their stories of drug addiction, sexual promiscuity, divorce, loss of loved ones, or struggles with infertility. "Compared with these," she said, "my life feels easy and less significant." She even admitted that she felt so embarrassed by the happiness of her story that she made up lies about herself to seem more mysterious and desirable to the "bad girls" in her church, a group painfully reminiscent of the cool kids in her high school lunchroom.

I was one of those bad girls. While Christina felt too good to be used by God in any meaningful way, I felt too sinful to be used at all. I believed I had too much sin in my past to be significant to God, while Christina felt as though she didn't have enough sin to be significant to people.

Turns out that despite our different stories, we had similar hearts—prideful ones. Satan was using the same sad, overdone lie on both of us: "You're not worth it, ladies. God doesn't want you." And that pride—my self-loathing, her self-pity—positioned both of us in the same, sad reality: stuck in the wrong story.

THROUGH THE BACK DOOR

It goes without saying that few people show up for their own story shakedown.

God knows this. So he knocks on the back door of our lives when we least expect him. He shows up without calling first. He walks straight on in to our houses, disregarding the five loads of

unfolded laundry scattered everywhere, the dirty dishes overflowing the sink, and the unidentified smell coming from the fridge.
Right there in the middle of our overpacked schedules and looming
deadlines, he audaciously asks one, simple thing: "Eat with me?"

"Look! I stand at the door and knock. If you hear my voice and
open the door, I will come in, and we will share a meal together as
friends" (Rev. 3:20 NLT).

This is how God interrupts our stories. Through the back door.

We expect and prepare for an entry through the front door.
Our front door is what people see when they look at us, the first
impression we are able to control and change. But the back door,
well, it's the least likely entrance to our homes. We don't expect a
knock around back where we've been stuffing all our junk for years.

Because knocks at the back door catch us off guard, we are disarmed and vulnerable. If God approaches there, in the least likely
part of our stories, he has a better chance of bypassing the preju-
dices and preferences we ask others to walk through to get to us.

God knows what we are still learning, that connecting our *why*
to our *what* is not only a lifelong process but a brutal one. Slowly
prying our white-knuckled grasp from our desire to be God is so
painful. Because we really love control. We love setting expectations. We love to say, "I'm fine. Nothing to see here."

So he starts slowly and with something we will easily get on
board with. "Hey," he says to us, "got anything to eat? An old box
of mac-n-cheese, some peanut butter and jelly, a freezer-burnt bag
of fake chicken? I'll take it! I just want to sit with you. I want nothing more than to hear you talk and watch you eat in an honest,
everyday place."

He tells his story by first engaging ours.

Throughout our lives, God tenderly approaches the rawest
places of our souls in a way that overturns our offenses, dismantles
our defenses, and slows down our brains long enough to connect

our thoughts to our feelings to our actions. He expertly crafts the most loving approach to our personal boundaries as he slowly chips away the lies we have grown to love.

God has written a story to reveal himself to us and make us whole again. He wants to tell us the truth—about him and about us. He wants to give us the chance to live with all of our doors and windows wide open, no room hidden, darkened, or closed off.

This is why not one painful, difficult, boring, or embarrassing moment is meant to be forgotten but instead is to help us remember a God who has been standing at the door of our hearts all along, knocking and calling.

There's no need to pick the place up. Don't waste your time cleaning, organizing, or minimizing. He doesn't need a fancy meal or the most expensive wine. He just wants you. All of you. Right where you are, the honest, first-draft version of you. All of your doubts, your curse words, your secret thoughts, hidden agendas, stuff you regret and are unsure about—he wants those too.

Do you hear him knocking? I know, he came around the back way. You weren't ready for him. But that's okay. Who wants to serve a God you can expect?

Go ahead. You can open the door.

Okay, fine. I'll go first.

> **God doesn't waste our stories. But he does want the real ones.**

CHAPTER 3

Starched Shirts and Supernatural Sightings

ABOUT THE TIME OF MY THIRTEENTH BIRTHDAY, MY PARENTS' divorce was finalized. Prior to that, it had been a long, turbulent home life with my dad in and out and my mom trying to decide which scenario she liked better.

My parents, high school sweethearts, lived on young love and our weekly, backyard parties full of cheap beer, faded denim, and loud Ronnie Milsap songs. But there's nothing like a screaming baby and a first mortgage bill to crash a good party.

I didn't realize we were poor until my fifth grade year when Allie Stuckey and Jade Kline told me it was gross that I'd worn the same shirt to school twelve times in three weeks, shoving their pencil-scratch record into my chest. I can still see my hands unfolding the crumpled piece of notebook paper marked with dates and tally marks. It was the first time that I'd thought about the fact that we drove twenty minutes to school while they walked merely the block from their homes. It was the first time I was so keenly aware that Allie's dad wore a shirt with her last name on it and that Jade's last name was plastered on billboards around town.

My dad wore a shirt with his name on it too. His first name, not his last. Suddenly, it was nauseatingly clear just how different our families were.

That day, I went home, threw my "gross" shirt in the trash, and asked my mom to *please* take me shopping. She took that opportunity not only to respond with a hearty no to the shopping but also to break my heart with the news that I wouldn't be returning to my private school the following year, the place I'd spent nearly every day of my life since prekindergarten.

I cried inconsolably for seven days. I made myself sick, cut my old "poor girl" shirts to shreds with scissors, and used that same pair of scissors to cut my forearm for the first time. Making myself bleed seemed to be the only pain I *could* control.

The only group of people who'd ever felt consistent and normal to me were at that school. I resented my little sister for being born and soaking up the extra money that once covered my tuition. I resented my dad for doing whatever he'd done to force Mom to kick him out. But I resented my mom the most. I didn't even know why. Maybe it was her seeming ambivalence toward my feelings. Most certainly it was because she was the only one there to resent.

Our childhood home was a 24/7 survival, every man for himself, just deal with it, pull yourself up by your bootstraps kind of environment. It was full of constant noise and stress. We all moved from one load of laundry to another, just praying the electricity would not go out this month like it did last month.

My dad was, and still is, the hardest working man I've ever known. He is devoted, loyal, and gives 110 percent to every task set before him, whether it be mowing the yard in precise three-foot rows or being hoisted thirty feet in the air to repair a transformer that had enough voltage to stop his heart with one slip of the hand. His job was hard and dangerous. At the end of the day, the last thing he needed was a houseful of annoying kids asking him to help with homework.

So he stayed away. Some days only as far as the driveway, tinkering with Old Yeller, his beloved two-tone-yellow '88 Chevy truck. Most of the time, however, it was the deer lease or a neighbor's back porch. He'd come home late in the evenings once we'd all gone to bed. I'd lie awake down the hall, crinkling my forehead to help me hear better. I wanted to know my father. To understand what or who made it difficult for him to be around us. So I'd try to listen to their arguments, sometimes pressing my ear against the wall and jotting down "important notes" in my bedside journal. Often the fighting stopped as quickly as it began. Soon after, the silence was diffused by the blaring television, maybe *Cheers* or *Thirtysomething*, neither of which we were allowed to watch. Other times, I would hear something crash or thud into the wall. Those sounds scared me. I'd scurry back to bed and squeeze my eyes shut, forcing myself to sleep.

The more frequently my dad stayed away, the farther out of reach our mom became, emotionally and physically. Often she secluded herself in her bathroom or sneaked a wine cooler to the patio. I'd never seen my mom cry, so her tough exterior was nothing new, but something about her *was* different. The day she told me we were too broke to pay tuition, I'd never seen her so lifeless. Without even a nod of compassion or an affirming pat on my shoulder, she simply turned and walked away. Not in a cold, calloused sort of way. More like an athlete who'd trained her entire life for a game she'd just lost. Her shoulders slumped, her skin was pale, her teeth yellowing, and dark purple circles under her eyes aged her beyond her years.

She looked defeated. Mostly, she looked sad.

Because Mom was the primary caregiver, her sadness set the tone for the entire house. Before long, we were all sad. Our home felt dark and suffocating.

By the time the divorce was official, my siblings and I were relieved. We craved normalcy, rhythm, and a lower decibel volume in communication.

My mom coped with single motherhood on the high side of depression—anxiety, busyness, sleepless nights, a cigarette when she thought no one was looking. My dad, however, spiraled rapidly to the low end—sadness, festering rage, withdrawal, a drink when he thought no one was looking.

There was nothing right or normal about the camper parked in the middle of a five-acre field we were forced to visit every other weekend. Dad had not been truly present in our first home, and he was not fully present in this one either. Whatever his part in Mom's decision, he seemed to take the divorce harder than she did. Sometimes I even felt sorry for him, glancing at him over my shoulder from my sister's diaper-changing station, watching as he poured himself another shot of whiskey.

Sometimes he forced himself to sit silently with us on the sofa and watch cartoons. But I was happier the afternoons he went outside and milled around on the lawnmower. His presence felt unnatural and stifling. The only times he seemed jovial or glad to be our father coincided with an empty sink, a picked-up bedroom, or a tucked-in shirt.

One weekend I'll never forget, Dad approached me with a favor. He wanted me to talk to my mom on his behalf and beg her to take him back. I was thirteen. And I was shocked! For days I contemplated his request. I'd never considered the possibility that *I* wielded enough power to reunite my parents. I assumed this ability should feel exciting and anticipatory of a new, better future. Instead, it felt unbelievably burdensome. If I had the power to bring my parents back together, had I also the power to divide them in the first place? At the worst possible time in a girl's hormonal history, I was contemplating the worst possible scenario: perhaps all of this—the fighting, the divorce, the drinking, the sadness—had been my fault.

When I finally asked my mom to remarry Dad, it took her all of five seconds to grab the phone and lay in to him. The familiar expletives gave me a sigh of relief, because I didn't want them back together, and I hated him for making me responsible for the possibility. At thirteen, those were the two things, the only things, I knew to be true.

It was, of course, all that I did not know that haunted me for years to come.

For example, I did not know that the groundwork of my identity had been laid through my parents' inattention, my mom's sadness, and my father's unfair expectations. At thirteen, I did not realize that years of constantly readjusting to my caregivers' ever-changing needs substantially delayed my developing healthy ways to address my own needs. And I certainly did not know it would take me twenty years to believe I was a beloved and not a burden.

I was ecstatic when my age finally caught up to the maturity that had been required of me my whole life. At fifteen, I received my driver's license and, more important, optional weekends with Dad.

More often than not, I still showed up for the previously court-mandated "every other," but only because my sister was five, my brother was twelve, and I wanted to protect them from Dad's mood swings. Both my parents spanked us when we disobeyed or rebelled, but back then, that was normal disciplinary parenting. The problem is, shame impairs rational thoughts, blame impairs rational behavior, and alcohol? Well, alcohol makes the irrational seem rational.

And all of us, my parents included, were really just kids in need of serious discipline.

One weekend in particular, hormones and selfishness got the best of me. I spent the night at my boyfriend's house, and when I attempted to sneak in undetected at the crack of dawn, my dad was on the sofa waiting for me. Turned out neither one of us had slept that night.

CREEKSIDE ANGEL

My mom unknowingly taught me how to channel my fear into rage for self-preservation. Therefore, I rarely cried. Even when nursing welts left on the back of my thighs by the slap of a leather belt, as I would do for the next few weeks, I would grind my teeth to powder before relinquishing pesky tears. So when my five-year-old sister rounded the corner into the living room to find me back-kicking into my dad's shins between blows, my fear pulsated into the anger of a protector.

Karly looked just like I did as a baby, but with the curliest thick, pitch-black hair toddlerhood has ever seen. Sucking her middle and ring fingers, she stumbled sleepily into the living room that early morning, rubbing her eyes and holding her pillow tight against her cheek. I darted away from my dad and scooped her up, tucking her safely behind the hideous brown-and-green-plaid sofa and unleashing a scream so violent and loud, it shocked my dad three steps backward.

"You touch her and I'll *kill* you!"

Something about her innocently stumbling onto the scene made me snap. Perhaps it was my lost childhood haunting me, reminding me just how fleeting innocence had been for me and how desperately I wanted it back. Maybe I was finally old enough to be aware that somewhere along the way, loathing him had morphed into loathing myself. I had loathed myself a few hours earlier slipping out of the arms of a drunken boy I barely knew, and I loathed this man who stood before me, a man I barely knew.

I raged through the house, my sister hiding behind the couch, shrieking for me to hold her. The louder she got, the more aggressive I became—knocking over lamps, breaking mirrors, kicking in walls.

That morning, I stood outside myself watching as I tucked

Karly safely into her bed with a movie, stomped out the back door, and ran toward the edge of the creek bed. Normally, I would have sped away in the torn upholstery seat of my red, four-door 1993 Buick Century, a hand-me-down from my grandmother. But today, an unseen force pulled me toward a smooth, large rock nestled beneath an overhanging oak that shielded it from the new morning sun.

My dad's house is built atop a steep hill. His back yard feels like one, long drop to the creek below. The water in the creek barely moves. It trickles ever so slowly through rocks and fallen trees. My dad had purchased the house post-divorce, so I had zero nostalgia attached to any of it.

As I sat on the rock, it was as if the reluctant water spoke to me. "It's safe here. You can cry with us."

As I cried for what seemed like days, a terrifying image unfolded in my mind—a picture of me sitting in my Buick inside my dad's closed garage, blaring my favorite album, *A Boy Named Goo*, breathing in the fumes. A smirk spread across my face as I imagined how bad he would feel that I died right there in the middle of his divorced-dad collection of tools and tarps.

I had never gone this dark before. Panic washed over me because the thought almost felt rational. Had I just formed a suicide plan?

I squeezed my eyelids together hard to force the vision out of my mind. I remember feeling afraid, alone, ashamed, and just crazy enough to do it.

Suddenly, a chill ran down my spine, forcing me to catch my breath and open my eyes. Not twelve feet in front of me stood the form of a human draped in radiant, white light. No gender to speak of. No identifying marks or clothing. Just palpable, pure light that spoke to my heart without saying a word.

It stayed only a few seconds. I remember feeling as though I'd known it forever. Its presence comforted me in the chambers of my heart. It seemed to communicate strength and grief at the same time. It took my breath away. I could feel my natural inclination to run away or to be paralyzed by fear settle into a sense of comfort and belonging I had never known before.

For one very brief moment in my big, chaotic world, I felt seen, wanted, and understood.

Then it was gone.

I'm not the only one who has seen what the Bible calls ministering spirits sent to serve us and spirits commanded by God to guard all our ways (Heb. 1:14; Ps. 91:11). Over the years, I've been surprised by how many people are not surprised by my angel sighting. I can't explain why I know for sure it was an angel, but I am one million percent confident it was. It was as real to me as the tiny hairs on my skin, which all stood at attention at the sight.

The memory of angelic accountability later haunted me out of some seriously rebellious teenage choices. More important, it was enough to convince me not to take my life. Although my circumstances did not take a drastic turn for the better, for that one supernatural second, I felt connected to something greater than myself.

My small trickle of hope felt just like that water in the creek— barely moving, but still there.

THE BEAUTY OF BUTTON-UP SHIRTS

I was a grown woman before I thought of my angel again. But in the weeks after the secret of my affair broke loose, it was all I could think about.

"Please, God, if you love me, show it to me one more time!" I begged and pleaded for one more reminder, one more fragment of hope, one more sign that my life would be missed.

In the moments after my epic belly laugh, I did what any good

Baptist woman does in the face of impending disaster. I tidied up a bit.

Now that the truth was out, I was strangely excited to confess everything to Justin.

In the hour before his arrival home from work, I calmly dressed Emma Grace in her pink polka-dot romper and Lake in his dinosaur onesie for a visit to their grandparents' house. After the two-minute there-and-back across the street, I freshened up. I took a shower, put on makeup, teased my hair, made the bed, and vacuumed the floor. I remember even spraying perfume around the room for added sensory effect.

When Justin walked through the kitchen into the living room, I was poised on the edge of our perfectly fluffed sectional, ankles crossed and hands folded delicately in my lap. I maintained my cool just long enough for him to unbutton the top button of his pristinely starched work shirt. But by the time he reached for the second button, I was sobbing hysterically.

Justin is a die-hard creature of habit. Every morning of our marriage he woke up early, took a shower, put on his starched pants and button-up shirt, grabbed a protein shake, and was out the door before I knew the world was turning. I would see him again around 5:30 p.m. He'd return home with a smile after a full day selling insurance.

In a well-choreographed dance, he gave a swift, one-handed unbuttoning down the front of his shirt, masterfully slipped out of it, and hung it by the shoulders on the back of the closest chair in record-breaking time.

Every day was the same—a small routine, but one that comforted me with its normalcy. Every night, no matter what event or task required our attention, I always found his perfectly starched and ironed button-up hanging on the chair long after he'd fallen asleep in the recliner watching the ten o'clock news.

A night owl, I was always up late organizing, reading, dreaming, gabbing on the phone, and at some point I would begrudgingly hang Justin's shirt in the closet, cursing him under my breath for not doing it earlier.

He and I have always been different this way. I, looking for the next rush of change. He, content to wear the same shirt seven times before washing it.

The Lord knew I would need a man like this—cool, constant, committed to rhythm and crisp button-up shirts.

I don't remember exactly what I said when he walked in other than "I'm sorry" every other sentence. I had rehearsed my confession hundreds of times. But when the moment came time, no part of me was prepared. Justin sat on the edge of the sofa across from me, elbows resting on his knees, never breaking his gaze, as though he'd been preparing for this his whole life.

I sucked in just enough air between sobs to release another incohesive string of thoughts at rapidfire pace.

"It's been on and off for three years . . . We were just friends, then . . . *Please* don't leave . . . Yes. I love him, *but*, I love *you*. I mean, I don't know . . . I'm confused. *How* could I do this to Rachel? . . . *our kids?!* I'm *so* sorry! I hate myself! *Who am I?!*"

Ten minutes into a three-year highlight reel that would tempt even Hugh Hefner's stomach to turn, I was abruptly cut off when Justin jolted from his seat and ran to the bathroom. A few moments later, he reappeared, drenched in sweat, red in the face, and weeping the most masculine, silent tears I had ever seen. I had seen Justin cry only once in nine years of relationship—at my stepfather's funeral. Even then, it was a "watering of the eyes after peeling an onion" kind of cry.

But in this moment, he felt so overcome with emotion that it forced him to vomit.

I had never felt more ashamed, more disgusted with myself,

more powerless. The time for laughter had come to an end. Now was the time for mourning. And grief settled hard into the fine lines and wrinkles of our starched and tidy little family. Barely a word was spoken between the two of us during the next three weeks.

Justin was different, but present. I could tell he was mostly in shock and, if only for survival purposes, staying put until he could identify some thread common to the life he thought he had been living and the one he really was.

Every now and then, I caught him standing on the back porch staring at our hay pasture, or wiping a tear from the corner of his almond-shaped blue eyes while he washed the dishes and didn't know I was looking. His shoulders slumped when he walked. His face was always sad. The once kind, boisterous, loud, aptly nick-named Governor of a cowboy who never met a stranger was now quiet, solemn, and broken.

I had broken him.

I didn't dare ask if he was leaving. Every now and then I asked him if he had any questions or how I could help him process. Some evenings I'd just burst into the bedroom after he'd been sleeping for hours and blurt out a confession of another adulter-ous memory. It drove me crazy that I couldn't remember episodes clearly enough to put in chronological order for him, even though he'd never asked for details in the first place.

Strange how our brains both protect and destroy us. I wanted to wash my hands of every memory with Ty, but I didn't want to let myself off the hook too soon. I needed to say it *all*. And I wanted to say it *now*, spew the poison inside me before it corroded one more cell.

I did my best to concentrate and answer what I assumed to be his biggest questions: How far did it go? Where would we go? How could I do this? What did I hope would happen now?

Most of the time, Justin responded only with the fact that his eyes were open. Other than that, he lay there, still and silent, until I said my piece and walked away.

Each morning that I woke up to him still lying there, I exhaled a sigh of relief. For all I knew and expected, at any moment I could walk in to find our closet depleted of button-up shirts.

As much as I wanted to, I didn't probe or push him to speak. I tried not to hold eye contact for too long either. Every now and then my heart skipped a beat when he reached out to touch my arm. I kept wondering if his touch would be enough to convince him (and me) that I hadn't ruined our entire life together.

As the days dragged on, I found myself wandering through the house late into the night, sobbing, tracing my finger over frames of family photos, pleading for just a sliver of supernatural light to crack through the walls of our home.

As I sat there alone at our kitchen table, white-knuckling the chair back, I begged God for just one more chance to hang up a button-up shirt.

> God doesn't waste our cries for help. He uses them to remind us it is good that we exist.

CHAPTER 4

Too Tired to Fight

KING DAVID, AN ADULTERER HIMSELF, WAS WELL-ACQUAINTED with a hopelessness so strong that it overwhelmed him "like a burden too heavy to bear" (Ps. 38:4). Elijah knew what it was like to spend alone time in the wilderness for fear of people, proclaiming, "I have had enough, Lord. . . . Take my life" (1 Kings 19:4). Jonah had a whale of a time in isolation and an even greater frustration on the outside when he declared, "Now, Lord, take away my life, for it is better for me to die than to live" (Jonah 4:3). Even Job, one of the most righteous men to walk the planet, must have questioned whether his life was necessary when he cried, "Terrors overwhelm me . . . my life ebbs away; days of suffering grip me. Night pierces my bones; my gnawing pains never rest" (Job 30:15–17).

But anyone whose anguish is so immense that it causes them to sweat blood, *that* person is quite familiar with the darkest night of the human soul.

> "My soul is deeply grieved to the point of death" . . . and [Jesus] fell to the ground and began to pray that if it were possible, the hour might pass Him by. And He was saying, "Abba! Father! All things are possible for You; remove this cup from Me; yet not what I will, but what You will."
>
> —MARK 14:34–36 NASB

And being in agony He was praying very fervently; and His
sweat became like drops of blood, falling down upon the ground.

—LUKE 22:44 NASB

We find Jesus at his weakest moments when he is alone: at
both the beginning and the end of his public ministry. Days away
from revealing himself to the first disciples, he was exhausted and
weary after forty days and nights of fasting in the wilderness. And
days away from his death, he felt grieved enough to beg God to
change his circumstances.

In both cases, despite his loneliness, grief, pain, perhaps
frustration, Jesus, unlike me, knew better than to engage in conversation with a liar while his resources were depleted.

While Jesus was in the wilderness and at his weakest, Satan
challenged Jesus to prove himself useful: "turn these stones to
bread." To show himself loved: "test God and see if he rescues
you." To prove himself worthy: "claim what is rightfully yours."
(See Matt. 4:1–11.)

In the garden or in the wilderness, the enemy's lie never changes.

Satan knows good and well that devoted believers will not turn
on a dime. No one who has experienced salvation enjoys crafting a
plan to distrust God. Satan knows that sincere Christians love God,
so much so that they will do just about anything to help him.

So Satan studies the lives of the genuine. He takes notes on
you like he took notes on me: (1) neglected in childhood, (2) strong
protector-fixer instinct, (3) questions value because of parents'
divorce, (4) willing to compromise for acceptance, (5) uses anger
to mask fear.

All of these made me the perfect candidate for a tsunami-sized
moral failing, someone willing to risk anything if it means securing
someone to love her everything.

Once I made the compromise for control in my life, all the

enemy needed to do was wait—prowl around the pitfall of my pride, a trap of his own design, until I was weak enough and isolated enough to engage him in conversation.

Somewhere in my loneliness and shame, my love for God became the excuse to distrust him, convincing myself that for my husband, children, friends, family, and, ultimately, God, life would be better if I was no longer in it. That's how Satan seduces us: he subtly and progressively distorts our thinking until we believe our sinning is for the sake of others.

Usually, we have no idea we've been kept in a custom chokehold for months, maybe years. This whole time, we thought we were wrapped in a security blanket.

> The seduction of Satan's lie—justifying our sin for the sake of others.

OUR SECURITY SNARES

"The fear of man lays a snare, but whoever trusts in the LORD is safe" (Prov. 29:25 ESV). The Hebrew word for "snare" in this passage is the same as "trap," which is used for hunting and catching.

Think about that word picture for a moment. A good trap, one intended to catch something, is designed with much skill by the hunter, often camouflaged and hiding in plain sight. Also, a trap is designed to lure, using something desirable as bait to draw in its victim. Finally, a trap closes shut around its prey, but oftentimes only wounding it without outright killing it. The trap will give just enough freedom for its prey to flail, claw, and fight without being released, leaving the prey to exhaust itself into a paralyzed state.

This is what it feels like to lie in Satan's snare.

The trap, personalized for our behaviors and built with much time and expertise, creates the illusion of security, the feeling that life inside the trap is safe, predictable, controlled.

The bait: praise of man. The one lure so irresistible that we rarely notice the subtle shift from our serving for God's glory to securing that glory for ourselves.

We don't realize that the scent of earning, performing, or striving should tell us the trap is near.

We feel the sting when its jaws clamp hard on our souls whenever our lives enter extremes; we become like wounded animals, flailing in the highs and lows of self-preservation. Highs like overeating, overtalking, overcommitting, overspending, overspiritualizing. Lows like isolation, mind-numbing consumption of media, mind-altering addiction, self-pity, apathy toward important relationships and events.

Bondage always reveals itself in the extremes of our lives, behaviorally and emotionally.

To be clear, fear is normal. We all experience it. God equipped our brains with self-preservation instincts to warn us of danger or harm. If a car barrels toward us, we *should* be scared and run away.

> **Bondage always reveals itself in extremes.**

If a relationship is verbally or physically abusive, fear should push us to seek help. If we remember the compromise we made that one night, fear of painful consequences teaches us not to do that stupid thing again.

Reasonable short-lived fear is a survival gift from God. But fear of the rejection or judgment of man will destroy us.

This is why God tells us that "fear has to do with punishment, and whoever fears has not been perfected in love" (1 John 4:18 ESV).

God offers us a perfect love, a love without condition. Because his love needs nothing from us, it is perfect. When we receive his love, we are free to love others perfectly, without need. Attempting to love or to receive love from others without first receiving God's perfect love will always end badly for us.

This is why rejection, abandonment, neglect, or distancing because we cannot meet a standard feels like punishment, like death.

Want to test me on this?

Think of a time when your love was rejected because you could not meet another's spoken or unspoken expectation. Think about that person who always seems to need something from you—an acknowledgment, an invitation, an apology, attention, your living on their terms.

Do these relationships feel light and free, or heavy and hindered? Do you find yourself drawing near to these people, or do you try your best to avoid them without hurting their feelings?

Maybe you've experienced this in a parent-child relationship when it feels like you can never do enough to earn favor. Or perhaps in a dating or spousal relationship when your partner's insecurities feel so vast that you cannot possibly fill them, even on your best day.

The conditions we build for love lurk in both the intentional and the unintentional: a passive-aggressive comment, a shift in tone or posture, a sudden or slow withdrawal, faking it, withholding affection to maintain control, or giving affection to get what we want.

Conditional love sucks, and it sucks the life out of us and others. People punish us whenever they serve their love with a side of expectation. And we punish others whenever we serve our love with a side of contingency plan.

We may be giving them our best selves, all of our honesty, affection, and energy. But we give unconditional love only when we release them from our expectations.

Unconditional, perfect love is rare because of the enormous amount of self-assessment and self-denial it requires. To love others as God loves us demands daily, sometimes hourly, self-examination of motive and intent, a constant self-check that we have not stumbled back into our security snares.

Perfect love is all we want in life, yet giving and receiving it doesn't come naturally to us. To receive it, we must never stop asking ourselves hard things. To give it, we must stop asking such hard things of others.

Acceptance, vulnerability, trust, no expectations, no games. This is what we want from people—to feel safe with our love and honesty. To confess our worst-case scenario without being rejected and to say out loud the worst thing we've ever done without it being used against us.

But we will never find complete safety in people.

Humans are not designed to carry each others' weight like this. Contrary to one of my favorite lines from the movie *Jerry Maguire*, you do not complete me.

Human relationships are designed to disappoint us. They are a setup by God to lead us right where he wants us: to the end of ourselves and others.

This is where you'd find me when I finally reached for God's grace: chasing the high of acceptance like a junkie, crashing hard and destroying myself for the next hit. Although God had released me from the trap long ago, there I sat crying and flailing about like a victim. Free to run, play, and enjoy life again, yet soothing my self-loathing with a lie.

> **Human relationships are designed to disappoint us.**

Why did I cheat on my husband? Because I loved my lie more than I loved God. It was my comfy-cozy security snare.

THE SAD LANDS

Over the course of three weeks postconfession, the silence and solitude I experienced slowly chipped away at the freedom I felt after receiving Ty's call.

For years, my life had been full-throttle noise. I had been constantly on the hunt for enough chaos to keep my secret covered, juggling the real and the fantasy, blurring lines so often that my dizzying spin could be calmed only by the next milligram higher amount of whatever I could talk my doctor into prescribing.

In twenty-one days, I received five "we can't be friends anymore" emails, made a handful of unreturned phone calls, and had one brief response to my "Can we talk?" text to Rachel: "I have nothing to say to you right now." Justified and open ended. Those are the worst. "So you *will* have something to say to me at some point?" I thought. "Can you just say it now so I don't have to rehearse everything you *might* say to me in the unforeseeable future?"

This is where the darkness began. With every note of rejection, more painfully with every note unresponded to, I crawled back into the front seat of my '93 Buick.

I hadn't spoken a word to anyone since my nauseating replay for Justin. He for sure had not said anything, which left only one option: our story was at the mercy of the other half of the "not so dreamy team."

I was back to my hormonal teenage self, trapped in the undertow of my parents' divorce, with extreme feelings and thoughts surging through my mind with nowhere to land.

I had so many words, but no voice to say them. I was the one with blood on my hands. No one wanted to hear what *I* had to say. And the only person who knew exactly what I was going through was off limits to me.

For the second time in my life, I felt truly alone with no power to change the situation.

David, Elijah, Jonah, Job, even Jesus had something in common with me in this moment. We were alone and at the mercy of others. Some by choice, others by consequence. Some, like Job, alone in a crowd of people.

God often requires of us a time of solitude in the aftermath of repentance. This is healthy. Going to church, serving in ministry, hanging with Christian friends, listening to worship music and online sermons might help keep our feelings in check and behaviors on track for a time. But even these good things can become the collective chaos helping to keep our lies on a loop.

Rushing through a life of routine does nothing more than teach us to practice what we think is true, but God wants us to know his truth as our reality. Normal life rarely helps us apprehend reality. Because God wants us to believe and hold his Word as our truth, not as a mere concept, he will use our experiences and relationships to force us off center, push us out of the rhythm of our comfort and into the quiet secret, sacred spaces of our hearts.

There is no better place than the wilderness, a brief season of solitude, to reset and relearn.

When slowing ourselves down is required to trust God more, nothing stops us dead in our tracks quite like the judgment of other people. God knows what we so quickly forget: desire cannot be tamed, only satisfied. As long as we find comfort in control, we will never surrender our need to him. Then one day, we will find ourselves at the end—weary, exhausted, master of nothing, mastered by everything.

Desire cannot be tamed, only satisfied.

I had so much noise in my head, years of lies and self-sabotaging patterns that felt like home. I had so busied myself with the things of God that I completely missed him. It was time for a serious downshift. My normal had to come crashing down if I were to take hold of facts and no longer be manipulated by my feelings.

Solitude was forced upon me. A time for me to test my core beliefs against the Word of God and decide which ones were real.

It makes sense that solitude and sadness walk hand in hand. I believe they are meant to. David was meant to use his solitude to grieve his rebellion against God. Elijah needed space to lament his intense fear of the judgment of other people. Jonah needed a minute to be mad about it. Job used his sadness through suffering to try to understand more about God. And Jesus, well, he took his alone time to ask God if there might be another option for his future.

Solitude and sadness are key to knowing God and ourselves more deeply. In the aftermath of personal sin or wrongdoing toward another, our solitude and sadness are key indicators that our repentance is true and having its way with us. "The sacrifices of God are a broken spirit; a broken and contrite heart, O God, you will not despise" (Ps. 51:17 ESV).

A short period of alone time with the Lord is essential after a season of habitual moral compromise. Maybe we've been caught in a loop of lies or need time to soften the rough edges of our personality. Maybe it's an affair, a divorce, substance abuse, poor financial choices, or a season of self-indulgence that leaves ruin in our wake. Whatever the reason, take time away from your daily routine to be sad over your sin.

But notice I mention a *short* time away.

God's discipline is not like human discipline. Remember, people need something from us, especially after we've wronged them. But God doesn't. His discipline is never from a heart of punishment but only and always from love. While people use our moral failings to push us away, God uses them to draw us in.

This is so important for us to remember in the aftermath of our stupidity, especially when we hold positions of leadership in our homes, businesses, or churches.

Are you a leader who has covered your sin far too long? Take a step back. If you've been a good leader, your project and your people don't need you up front to keep things running. If you've done your job well, you can take a few weeks, maybe months or years, to step away from the machine long enough to grieve and repent with the Lord. The length of time you engaged in the sinful behavior may dictate the length of your break. Behaviors become habits over the course of two months, and those behaviors become a core belief over the course of two years. It takes about this long to break an ingrained habit or belief.

But don't let yourself stay away too long lest you miss the point of all this pain.

People may want you to sit this thing out forever. There may be voices, real or perceived, who prefer you never lead again, that you never experience success or happiness again. But these are people, not God. May we not confuse godly grief with worldly grief. Here's the difference: "Godly grief produces a repentance that leads to salvation without regret, whereas worldly grief produces death" (2 Cor. 7:10 ESV).

To test whether you are experiencing godly grief or worldly grief, ask yourself, Is it producing change? Godly grief is fruitful. It does not immobilize or impair us. It is temporary and effective. Godly grief turns our attitude around. It changes us from the inside out.

Coming to the end of our conceptual experience of God awakens us to his reality, which does nothing but inspire a genuine believer to live an obedient, risk-taking life. Oh, *please*, reader, I implore you, reject any teacher or message telling you not to feel sorry, guilty, or ashamed for your sin. We must feel all of these emotions, all the way to the end, if we are finally to live in victory over our sin.

Believing that we do not need to feel guilty only perpetuates our guilt.

You will know you've lingered far too long in solitude and sadness when your guilty conscience does not allow you to enjoy God's forgiveness. This is the warning sign, the alarm sounding to say, "Okay! Time. You've been here long enough. Now get up, go outside, walk around. Talk to someone, even if you have to pay them to listen to you, and serve again, lead again, do something again."

If you feel yourself sinking into depression, toying with dark thoughts of hopelessness and death, you have stayed too long in isolation. If you no longer feel joy over God's ability and desire to forgive you, you have made the dangerous, subtle shift from godly to worldly grief. The moment you feel too sad to receive God's grace is the moment you've gone too dark and stayed too long.

> Believing that we do not need to feel guilty only perpetuates our guilt.

I remember this place well.

After I had been three weeks in the wilderness of solitude, the silence left me just enough downtime for the perceived and stated judgment of others to deafen any hope I'd been listening to. Like the angry, exhausted girl by the creek bed, I saw no way forward. Who knows whether it was dozens of repressed memories triggered at one time or the seductive whisper of Satan enticing me to just stop fighting and go to sleep, but when the thought of ending my life flashed through my mind, no angel appeared to talk me out of it.

Once again, standing outside myself, squeezing my eyelids shut, shaking violently as the tiny, white rocks of "Kasey's desolate kingdom" filled my palm, the darkest night of my soul overtook me. Sadness, despair, hopelessness, shame, and fear mixed a cocktail of my prescription Xanax and a dusty old bottle of Jack Daniel's hidden in the back of our pantry.

My mind's eye found its way back to my dad's garage. Though I was twenty-nine years old, my fifteen-year-old self, with her stolen innocence, shame-laden pride, and paralyzing fear of rejection, still raged within.

But this time, she was just way too tired to fight.

JUSTIN'S WORST DAY

According to Justin, of all the days he has lived, his worst was not the day he learned his wife was cheating on him but the day she narrowly cheated death.

Three weeks after our world fell apart, I attempted to take my life with an overdose. Sincerely believing it was the most unselfish thing I had done in a while, and in a last-ditch effort to regain control over the painful truth that I was indeed not in control, the only part of that day I did think through was Justin's clocklike reliability.

After checking that both kids were sound asleep for their two-hour afternoon nap, I stood in the kitchen and stared at the last of my Xanax poured out on our dark countertop. I knew if I hesitated even for a moment I would chicken out. So, thirty minutes before Justin was sure to return home, I scooped up the pills, maybe twelve or fifteen in all, chunked them toward the back of my throat, and chased them with three large gulps of whiskey.

Collapsing to the floor in a sort of comatose anxiety attack, I laid there, weeping. Here I was once again on our beautifully-stained concrete floor, inches and miles away from those fleeting moments of freedom and laughter.

This time, no supernatural light need fill the room for chills to rush down my spine. What had I done? I didn't even know whether twelve pills would be enough, but within seconds of swallowing, I wanted them all back. I panicked. Heaving through sobs, I crawled to the phone nearby and fumbled Justin's number.

"Hey." He answered plainly on the first ring. "Almost there."

"Hurry! Please hurry!" I screamed.

"What's wrong?!" His voice now matched my tone.

"I'm so sorry, Justin. I'm just so sorry. I . . . I took my pills . . . a lot of them. I don't think it's enough . . . but I don't know. I'm sorry, just please come."

Click. Dial tone.

I propped my back against the trash compactor, dropped the phone, and, succumbing to drowsiness, breathed deeply through the trembling of every nerve in my body.

Darkness, like a blanket, enveloped me.

THE SETUP

That's the thing about angels. One can never be sure they haven't been there all along. "Do not neglect to show hospitality to strangers, for thereby some have entertained angels unawares" (Heb. 13:2 ESV).

I begged God for an angel.

And he sent one.

That day, in a move that can be described only as God's sovereign rule over our lives, Justin pulled in the drive about the time I blacked out. He raced inside, stuck his finger down my throat, and I purged. Had the pills not been counted, we would have rushed to the hospital. But I was coherent enough to nod "that's all of them." I stayed lucid long enough to convince us both that I was in the clear. Then I drifted under again to sleep off the remnants.

When I was moments from death, and while our children slept (because of the lullabies of their own angels, no doubt), my cowboy called Satan's bluff once and for all. "You intended to harm me, but God intended it all for good. He brought me to this position so I could save the lives of many people" (Gen. 50:20 NLT).

Satan meant to destroy me that day—not figuratively, literally. And he meant to dismantle our marriage, our children's future, and any semblance of peace one could hope for in life. Instead, God's grace and supreme control were put on display in his defeat. Through my shame, sin, and one horrific moment of despair, God's purpose for us was revealed.

As Justin and I learned, and as I hope to encourage you, reader, to see, nothing exists apart from the perfect will of God. Not the evil in this world, not our sin, not Satan's schemes, not a despairing wife's suicide attempt or a cowboy's schedule. Everything exists through Jesus, by Jesus, for Jesus, to show Jesus is exactly who he says he is (John 1:3; Heb. 1:2; Col. 1:16).

In AD 33, the worst sin ever committed—putting Christ to death—ultimately displayed God's glory. When Christ rose from the dead, the dark night of this world was finally and fully dismantled, bringing glory to the very thing Satan meant to destroy—the good will of God.

The same will be true for you.

Your life's dismantling—an addiction that leads you to rock bottom, a secret exposed, the loneliness that grieves you, the achieving that exhausts you, her rejection, his betrayal—all eventually will be seen for what they truly are—the *good* will of God.

"And we know that for those who love God all things work together for good, for those who are called according to his purpose" (Rom. 8:28 ESV).

Reading these words now, you may feel numb, useless, powerless, sidelined.

That's okay. God is using even this unlikely book, written by this unlikely girl, to remind you just how much he has in store for you.

If he can prove it to a hardheaded, lie-loving, people-fearing, harlot-hypocrite like me, he will prove it to you.

Our worst day, most horrific pain, and most desperate darkness *will* be used to the glory of God. Our lives are but a divine setup for us to be sure of this truth. Nothing that has happened to us or through us is a mistake or an accident. God takes no pleasure in our pain, but he does purpose it.

God is using the best and worst parts of us to make us whole. He doesn't just want our lives to be happy, peaceful, or blessed. It's better than that. He wants our lives to be full—mind, body, and soul all working together to choose his love more often, and faster than we did the first time around.

Yes, he does make us new, teaching us new ways to think, respond, and deal. But to make something, one needs materials. And not just any material. Raw, natural, specifically cut material.

Our story is God's raw material for the new thing he is building. This is why our past is not to be dismissed, downplayed, or undefined but instead is to be used as the resource to rebuild and restore us.

> God is using the best and worst parts of us to make us whole.

God is using our best and worst days to give meaning, design, and purpose to the whole of us.

I can't wait to show you.

God doesn't waste our darkest days. He uses them to point us toward the light.

CHAPTER 5

Attach: Did You or Didn't You?

THE FIRST TIME I LAID EYES ON JUSTIN, IT WAS LIKE WATCH-ing the iconic scene of John Wayne leaning in the doorway in *The Searchers*. Justin wore a cowboy hat low on his brow, and his skin was rosy and fair with youth, but his eyes, already forming tiny crow's-feet in each corner, made him look as if he'd spent eighty years on the open range drinkin' coffee, smokin' a pack a day, and talkin' about the weather.

With his collar upturned beneath a bright yellow rain slicker, Justin, a senior in college, leaned coolly against the carport wall of our college pastor's home. It was my first official college church party—the annual Halloween bash that had made a name for itself as the who's who of the predestined (or not, depending on how much cleavage your costume showed).

I, a freshman dressed as one of the Three Amigos (tassel pants, sombrero, the works), unashamedly shook my booty to the DJ's pathetic attempt to "redeem" a collection of Christian music hits by remixing in Jennifer Lopez's "Waiting for Tonight."

Rain hammered Justin right where he stood, streaming off the brim of his hat and pooling in the indentions of his poncho. The brisk cold front had finally brought a welcomed reprieve from our suffocatingly stale Texas summer. But the downpour didn't seem to faze Justin one bit. Stoically planted as the unofficial greeter, he casually chatted through the rain, welcoming incoming students with a half-cocked smile and a hat tip to the ladies.

Most everyone, myself included, thought it was all a part of his act, his cowboy costume. But I soon learned it was only Justin being Justin, dressed as he always dressed, behaving as he always behaved, oozing southern charm as thick as the syrup my gran called her sweet tea.

Justin had quite the reputation as a "lady's gentleman." He was certainly the only college student on campus who wore his cowboy hat and boots daily and to everything—football games, church, class, fundraisers, the pool. East Texas summers reach 110 degrees of the stickiest heat you've ever wanted to give up on life in, and yet there was the cowboy, sporting his shorts, tank top, boots, and a wide-brimmed hat.

Justin was also a member of the notorious Baptist boy's club on campus who called themselves, wait for it, the Chiquitas. An absurd backstory goes here, not at all involving bananas, so I won't waste your time. All you really need to know is that the Chiquitas were the college accountability group where freshman girls' wedding dreams went to die.

Only the most self-controlled Chiquita would rise in rank as the most desirable among the ladies, driving the *I Kissed Dating Goodbye* curriculum train to compromise or the altar, whichever came first. (Parents, if between the years of 1997 and 1999 you ever wondered why your young adult daughter never left her room or why she listened to the Goo Goo Dolls on repeat, it was because of this book.)

Once I learned that this group of do-gooders planned to kiss only the girl they would marry, I was intrigued. Okay fine, obsessed. But I was a far cry from fitting the Chiquita-groupie profile. I thought Wednesday hamburger lunches at the Baptist Student Ministry were a lame excuse for Christians to congratulate themselves on their tally of how many unassuming "lost" students they lured to a free meal. The only sorority letters I had to my name were "I-Smoka-Cig" and "I-Tappa-Keg." And I most certainly did not wish to kiss dating goodbye. I had kissed more boys than there were Chiquitas. It seemed irresponsible to wait until the altar to kiss. What if he was one of those wide-mouth kissers or a drooler or used too much tongue? I had no intention of using my "for better and for worse" on an incompatible kisser.

But if I was going to show up on the Chiquitas' radar, I had to put in my good-girl hours with the campus Christians. So I started with the costume party.

That night, as the cowboy's eyes met mine, I locked in on my target. I suddenly felt the urge to break him and expose his reformed gang of walking cliches for exactly what they were: regular boys who wanted to have sex.

Attractive, confident, the polar opposite of me, an upperclassman, Justin was so notorious as the model Chiquita member even I, a freshman on the outskirts, had heard of him. And now he was walking toward me.

"Howdy, Justin Van Norman. And you're Kasey Porter," he declared with an outstretched hand. Surprised that he knew my name, I gripped his hand to match his resolve and blushed in spite of myself.

"Yes, Kasey. And *you're* the cowboy I've heard so much about."

Now I wasn't the only one blushing.

UNATTACHED ANNIE

The fall I met Justin, I was knee-deep in a research paper for Behavioral Psychology that was due at the end of the semester. I titled it "Unattached Annie."

In my paper I referred to a study in which British psychologist Dr. John Bowlby follows three-year-old Annie, along with her parents, in the year 1948.

As many parents did at this time, Annie's mom and dad dropped her off for an extended stay at a London asylum for children with tuberculosis. Little did Annie's parents know, just as they were admitting their daughter, a curious young psychiatrist, Dr. John Bowlby, was visiting the sanitarium to gather data for his research on child-parent attachment.

Annie could be without her parents for weeks to months. And as they turned to leave the building, it was obvious that Annie did not understand what was happening to her. The moment Annie's mother turned away, Annie's face washed with confusion and distress as she began to cry. As Annie ran to grab hold of her mother's dress, a nurse restrained her. Over the next few days, regardless of how well the nurse attended her needs, Annie was inconsolable—throwing fits, beating her fists on the floor, crying and screaming.

Dr. Bowlby continued to observe Annie, as well as the other children who were being admitted to the hospital. He observed that each child responded to their parents' leaving the same way Annie did.

Dr. Bowlby named this stage of attachment theory "protest."

Several days later, Dr. Bowlby documented a significant change in Annie's mood. Instead of throwing fits of rage, Annie seemed to slip into a state of grief. She refused to play with other children, refused to eat, and moved lethargically around her room. The nurses, having seen this state many times before, seemed relieved to have a moment of rest from the child's rollercoaster emotions. When trays of food were placed in front of Annie, she pushed them away. When other children attempted to play dolls or to color with Annie, she refused to reciprocate, isolating herself in her room.

Dr. Bowlby classified this stage as "despair."

As Dr. Bowlby continued to observe Annie and the other children whose parents had now been absent for more than a month, he noticed another marked change in their mood. The children seemed to move into a new state of existing.

When the idea of her parents' continuing absence became a reality, Annie began to play with her friends, eat her meals, and compliantly respond to the nurses who were attending her. Annie enjoyed coloring and spent hours a day with her coloring pages. Her anger and depression had subsided. It seemed Annie had slipped into the rhythm of her new normal.

Until one Sunday afternoon when Annie's mother visited.

As Annie's mother approached, Annie's response shocked Dr. Bowlby and his associates. He'd expected Annie to be excited to see her mother return, perhaps jump into her arms and giggle. Instead, the opposite occurred.

Annie barely looked up as her mother walked toward her. As her mother leaned down to kiss her, Annie pulled away. Annie's next move shocked Dr. Bowlby once again. Annie slowly and carefully pushed her newly colored pages underneath the papers in front of her so that her mother could not see her latest masterpiece.

Dr. Bowlby called this stage "detachment."

In a matter of only a few weeks, Annie had detached herself from her mother.

After many subsequent years of research, Dr. Bowlby concluded that at only three-years-old, Annie knew that if she allowed her mother back into her life, she risked being hurt again. So, like the way she hid her drawing beneath her papers, Annie buried her need for trust, intimacy, and security. By hiding her drawing, Annie was communicating to her mother, "I can no longer trust you. You no longer have access to my love."

Like with all of us, Annie's core beliefs about her identity were established early in her childhood. While you and I most likely were not abandoned by our parents to an asylum, our views of God, others, and ourselves have been shaped by the proximity and pattern of the relationships that were available to us in the first few years of our lives.

Dr. Bowlby's research with Annie and other children led to groundbreaking discoveries in how adults relate to other adults based on how their parents related to them as children. For example, children whose parents were unlike Annie's—reliable sources of comfort and strength—have a lifetime of advantages compared with those whose parents were not present (either physically or emotionally).

Dr. Bowlby discovered that the more responsive a parent is to their child within the first three years of life, the more stable and secure the child will become as an adult, developing healthy ways to interact with other adults.

Like Annie, when we are rejected by those closest to us, we teach ourselves to attempt to replace the negative feelings associated with this pain with something we can control—use of time, work, a substance, money, a habit, another feeling.

The more frequently we experience rejection by those who should accept us (a parent, a spouse, the church), the more deeply we bury our need for trust, intimacy, and vulnerability with people in general.

By the time I met Justin, I was a twenty-year-old "unattached Annie" who hadn't just buried but suffocated her need for trust, intimacy, and vulnerability. Like Annie, the core beliefs of my identity were shaped by the rejection of those I wanted to love me most—my parents.

I "protested" as a loud, volatile young teen who screamed, slammed doors, and once punched her fist through a wall. I "despaired" as a shame-ridden young adult living a double life of daytime church girl, nighttime floozy. By the time one "detached" amiga met one attached cowboy, relationships to her were things to be observed, manipulated, and controlled.

My entire life, I had been hiding my desire to be fully loved. Entering my twenties, I had not only detached myself from the possibility of receiving love but also replaced the desire with things I could control—achievement, image, a man's sexual desire.

I had no intention of risking my love on anyone.

But I'd never met a real-life cowboy.[1]

JUST A SIDE HUG

There was no doubt about the zing of attraction between me and Justin the night of the costume party. Despite my fake mustache, Justin lingered closer to me as the night went on. We joked through lighthearted banter. Every now and then, I playfully reached to touch his biceps like something was funny.

I remember nodding flirtatiously into Justin's baby blues with a smirk, thinking, "You have no idea who you're dealing with, buddy."

Although I didn't have words for it at the time, I was displaying a key indicator of undealt-with hurt. Because misery loves company, undealt-with pain most often exposes itself in corresponding behavior toward others. If we feel like liars, we make it our mission to uncover the lies of others. If we feel neglected, we easily neglect others. If we feel betrayed, we are quick to turn on important relationships. In my case, in the pain of my sexual sin I wanted to expose the sin of the Chiquita boys. Because I didn't want to feel alone in the shame of promiscuity, I sought to unravel those who seemed unscathed by it.

There was no Chiquita ringleader to speak of, but there were a few who garnered more female clamor than others. One of whom was the cowboy himself.

And just my luck, not long after the Halloween party, I scored a job as the student intern for the First Baptist Church Christian Life Center. A fancy title for the person who schedules, cleans, and locks up after all the extracurricular church activities—wedding showers, food drives, senior adult aerobics, and most important for me, the weekly Chiquita accountability group.

I mischievously eavesdropped from behind a nearby Coke machine and laughed to myself as the ring of self-controlled saints boastfully reported on all the girls they had refrained from kissing each week.

What oafs. It took only one pass in my V-neck T-shirt to derail the entire meeting.

"Hey, guys," I said, offering my smoldering side-eye toward Justin. "Need anything? Temperature good in here?"

"Oh! Uh . . . yeah, Kasey, thanks! We're great!" Overcompensatingly cheerful as if their moms had just caught them looking at porn.

Maybe I saw it only because I wanted to, but I could have sworn Justin was laughing with me. Once we started dating, he told me that he never bought in to the whole "lip virgin" movement. But the fact that his girlfriend prior to me became an actual nun leaves this claim still up for debate.

Our first date was January 2, 2000, the night of one of the hardest freezes East Texas has ever seen. Though most roads were shut down and only one restaurant was open, the tension of desire between the two of us was hot enough to risk cold and possible death.

Justin and I gabbed through fifteen bowls of chips and salsa. Four hours flew by as if we'd known one another for years. Justin surprised me with the type of questions he asked. "Tell me about your mom. What's she like? How would your siblings describe you? When you get mad, then what happens?"

A young counselor in training, I was startled by how out of

line I'd been in my early assessment of him. Justin was not just some cowboy. He was kind, attentive, and genuinely interested in, well, *me*. I had never sat across from a man who had the nerve and self-awareness to ask me the questions that mattered. To be fair, my bold, feisty, passive-aggressive temperament never made it easy for anyone to know the real me. But something about Justin's demeanor disarmed me.

As the night went on, however, a few of my assumptions were confirmed. Justin had felt loved by his "still together" parents his entire life. Outside of losing his grandparents, he could not recall one specific trauma or hard time that he had endured. And he was a virgin, saving himself for marriage like all good Chiquita boys should. (And yes, I asked. My cold heart could not refrain. His, however, was warm enough not to return the question.)

I had never felt this way about a man. I had never felt this way period.

I was drawn in by Justin's steady, sure nature like a moth to the flame. His radical combination of innocence and confidence seemed to checkmate my game of guarded love.

By the end of the night, no exaggeration, I knew I would marry this cowboy. Especially when he walked me to the front door, took one step back, tipped his hat with a "thank you," and turned to walk back to his truck. I laughed out loud and shouted, "Justin! It's okay. You can at least give me a hug!"

I'll never let go of the image of that huge grin spreading across his bright red face as he turned back, slamming his palm into his forehead, and let out a "doh!"

I could barely contain my childlike state as he sheepishly walked back to hug me—but just a side hug.

As Justin's cute, Wrangler-wearing butt trotted away down the sidewalk, I leaned against the door and thought, "Maybe *I'm* the one who's in trouble here."

After only one night with Justin, my heart trembled at the prospect of a new option, an option the Annie in me never saw coming and never knew she wanted: a man who might love her not because it made sense to or because he needed something from her but just because he darn-well wanted to.

God wastes no relationship from our past but uses it to prove he is the only one always with us and for us.

74

CHAPTER 6

Parental Predisposition Problems

"Mom! Chill out. We were just . . . just . . . praying!"

"Are you kidding me?!" she shouted. "Who do you think you are?"

As my mother grabbed my shoulders hard enough to choke out the blood supply to my fingertips, her face turned fire-engine red and her bright green eyes darkened.

"But Mom," I pleaded, "you don't under—"

She shoved me into the wall before I could finish my sentence, plummeting her voice to a whisper and pressing her nose hard against mine. "Don't even think about telling me I don't understand. I understand just fine." Crescendoing so he could hear from the bedroom, she said, "You were having sex! In my house! Under my roof! Praying, my ass!"

With one hand still pinning me against the wall, she reached with the other for my bedroom doorknob. "No!" I gasped. Every muscle in her face now pulsating, she drove her pointer finger into my chest on each word. "Kasey. Don't. You. Move. Don't you say another word."

She swung open my bedroom door just as Tanner was buckling his belt.

"Get out of my house, Tanner!" she roared.

He ducked beneath her approaching saber-pointer and darted

past me without a glimpse, Mom chasing him down the hallway and out our front door.

"And if I ever catch you near my daughter again, I will . . . I will . . ." The sound of his Firebird engine starting up echoed in our blue-collar neighborhood. She cupped her mouth to make a megaphone. "It will not be good for you, young man! Not good at all!"

Tanner drove the only Camero in our 1200-student high school. It came in handy for him when he wanted to, you know, pray with girls.

A member of the Dragon High Prayer Team, Tanner learned early on that his tumultuous home life could be used as a pity play to get unassuming Baptist girls to lay hands on him, so to speak.

That's where I first met Tanner—prayer team. I was a charter member.

So the night he called me needing prayer, I knew what he really wanted. Although I had no intention of interceding on his behalf, I said, "Sure. Come on over. Mom's out of town." I felt a tad indebted, because the truth was I'd been using him too.

I was a sophomore, he a senior, and one slow, drive-by through the student parking lot in the passenger seat of his Camero earned me enough reputation credits to last for weeks. I had zero attraction to Tanner and even less desire to have sex with him. But something about riding in his car with the windows rolled down blaring the Beastie Boys felt liberating. It was a rush observing the expressions on the other students' faces as we rolled by: perplexed, intrigued, jealous.

My mom caught me and Tanner making out on my bed when she returned home early from a weekend getaway with Dave.

Dave was a truck driver she'd met months earlier at the only dance hall within fifty miles of our small town. All I knew about Dave was that he had a creepy mustache and had recently renovated the back cab of his semitruck to mimic some swanky Vegas suite he'd once visited.

Mom forced me to crawl in and take a look once. The whole thing made me want to throw up in my mouth.

His cab walls were draped in dark red velvet trimmed with gold tassel. A picture of Elvis (also velvet) darkened the only light available through the back window. And the ungodly number of colorful, flashy pillows he had piled in there made me wonder how anyone could experience a "what happens in Dave's truck, stays in Dave's truck" kind of moment. My hair and clothes down to my bra reeked of cigarette smoke for days.

By the time Tanner called, I was primed for mustache payback. I despised my mom for leaving me to manage my six-year-old sister and thirteen-year-old brother while she was off tossing velvet pillows with Dave.

Whether or not she would have caught us, I was a mere two seconds away from shoving Tanner off my bed after hearing him unlatch his belt buckle. As long as I was in control of how far it went physically with boys, I was fine. But tonight, I wouldn't get the chance to show Tanner who was really in charge of this prayer meeting. Instead, I spent the next three hours being scolded on my living room sofa, watching my mother pace and rant on and on about respect, rules, and how disappointed she, God, and the whole world were with me.

Finally, the consequence came—subjected to yet another weekend of babysitting my siblings while she explored her "healing journey" via Vegas on wheels. No shocker there.

STRETCHY GENES

We all have a fixed set of inherited genes within our chromosomes, but only a fraction of our genes will ever switch on. The ones that do, do so because of environmental messages they receive.

Which genes switch on depends on how we think about the world around us.

Research tells us that 75 to 98 percent of our mental, physical, and behavioral illnesses come from what we think about ourselves and others, leaving only 2 to 25 percent to be determined by our genetics. The meaning we assign to people and experiences over the course of our lives directs our DNA to turn on or off.[2]

As we grow, our thought patterns change who we are—minimizing or maximizing our likelihood of illness, addiction, or depression. No wonder God speaks through Paul to remind us we are transformed by the renewing of our minds (Rom. 12:2).

While our genetics may predispose us to a specific problem like aggressive behavior or anxiety, they do not produce the problem. Instead, what we think about the problem gives it power over us.

Our childhoods offer plenty of room for our genes to stretch what we experience into who we believe we are.

> While genetics may predispose us to a problem, what we think about the problem gives it power over us.

Aside from our physical appearance, my mom and I were as different as two people can be. My thick, dark hair, wide hips, sharp nose, and jawline confirmed our blood relationship. But that was about all that attached Krecia and me to one another.

She was messy, I was clean. She lived for the moment, I planned. She hoarded every paper ornament and school drawing since prekindergarten, I threw that kind of crap away.

We drove each other crazy with our differences, which kept us from verbalizing our love for one another. To this day, I can count on both hands how many times I heard my mom say she loved me. Each time it seemed that she was on the verge of saying it, she paused just long enough to talk herself out of it. As I got older,

I could see her eyes darting back and forth as she ran the cost-benefit analysis that stopped her short of saying the actual words.

She did her best to show us we were loved the only way she knew how—chaos.

Mom was no good at vulnerability, but she was great at creating mesmerizing distractions around intense feelings until you forgot that you were feeling in the first place.

When I was little, I often caught her crying alone in her bathroom. She would see me out of the corner of her eye, scoop me up, and plop me on the bathroom countertop with a "let's do your makeup, doll!" Acting as if I'd just stumbled into the punchline of a joke, she would say, "Would you just look at my mascara?! Why, I'm nothin' but a big, scary monster!" turning her voice deep and wriggling her fingers toward me for a tickle. A wide grin spread across my five-year-old face as her arms and hands magically removed every remnant of her true feelings, entertaining me at the same time.

"One rarely needs anything more in life than a pink tube of Great Lash mascara! It will never let you down, honey!" She leaned in, opened wide her mouth, and pretended to layer my lashes.

When I was seven and eight, I could expect pancake breakfasts with marshmallows and chocolate chips the morning after a deafening fight between her and Dad.

As a preteen, I could set my watch by the sound of Michael Jackson booming through our stereo speakers on Saturday mornings while Mom washed our car in the back yard, wearing denim cutoff shorts and using the water hose as a microphone. My brother, sister, and I would dance and sing along, for one moment forgetting that our world was falling apart.

Mom worked the same full-time job for eighteen years—head of new accounts at a bank. Each evening was a whirlwind of survival—laundry, homework, baseball, choir practice, my little sister throwing potty-training tantrums. We all scarfed down whatever cereal box Mom'd thrown on the kitchen table for dinner.

It went on like this my entire childhood—constant motion, noise, never quiet enough to hear ourselves think, much less talk. Mom, so full of life, energy, and fun, a woman beloved by her friends, the life of the party to anyone who knew her, yet a mystery to her children. Like watching a thrilling movie unfold was to be my mother's daughter, sitting on the edge of her seat.

The chaos and crazy of our lives kept serious conversations at bay. But children grow up and have questions about the movie, and one day need to write their own scripts.

Like the day I started my period in Mrs. Prince's seventh-grade theater class. Embarrassed and scared, I called my mom at work to ask her what to do. She responded by dropping off to the school secretary a brown paper sack full of tampons, with a smiley face and the words "Happy Woman Day!" written on the front in permanent marker.

I remember tucking the sack under my shirt so no one would see and frantically scanning the school lobby expecting her to be standing behind me snickering. Instead, she had already gone. She had never even taught me how to use a tampon. I didn't really understand why I was bleeding in the first place, and for a few months after that lived in absolute terror that I would spontaneously become pregnant.

I locked myself in the bathroom stall for the remaining two hours of school and wept into my favorite pair of jeans, which were now ruined and lying in a pile on the floor. With trembling hands, I fumbled through the awkward and painful gift of my "Woman Day" one piece of cotton after another.

That was the first time I remember feeling truly wounded by my mother.

Something about the shame of bleeding, the anger of not

knowing how to work a simple piece of cardboard and cotton, plus the feeling of being abandoned by the one person assigned to help me felt life altering.

Before this moment, I was aware of being sad and confused by the things going on in my family. Whether it was because of my lack of maturity or God's gift of protection, my family's dysfunctional patterns had been obscure, external, a movie I was forced to watch whether or not I wanted to. Until now, I had never questioned why all these bad things were happening—the fighting, the chaos, the unspoken tears, the divorce. Even as a child, I believed my mom and dad loved me. But not until this moment, clutching the porcelain and kicking at the stainless-steel box of my junior high bathroom stall, had I questioned whether I was wanted.

Suddenly, my brain was connecting my experiences with my feelings. Like the first flicker of a powered-on screen, a belief was coming online, changing my brain, switching on my DNA, morphing my experience into identity. A worldview was taking shape, one that could be modified by events but for now embodied my sense of self. From now on, all significant relationships would contribute their answer to the question, "Am I or am I not optional?"

OPTIONAL

Poor Tanner never returned to the Porter home. As a courtesy, I never again asked for a ride in his Firebird.

By the end of my junior year, Trucker Dave was long gone and Mom had married a quiet, kind man ten years her elder. Their decision to build a home that no longer required him to sleep in the same bed in which I was procreated meant moving us into a small, temporary camper-trailer during construction. The camper was so small it was missing an entire bedroom—mine.

The most shocking part was the ease with which Mom dropped the bomb on me.

"Kasey, do you think the Bennetts would mind if you lived with them while we build the house? I know it's your senior year and all, but we really just don't have the space in the camper. Besides, I know it's weird for you living with a stepdad."

The Bennetts made sense. I spent most of my time there anyway. Reverend Bennett was the music pastor at my church. He and his wife had taken me under their wing, offering me a job collating the choir folders each week and setting an extra dinner plate for me each night. His two daughters were my best friends, bookending me in age.

They were a wonderful family, just not mine.

I don't remember much of what Mom said next. As I'd done the night she caught me with Tanner, I shut down the painful reality that existed between us and stuffed my feelings somewhere deep inside.

Just like her, I could joke away hard things, turn sadness into sarcasm, fill awkward silence with a funny movie quote, entertain instead of engage. Already an expert pretender, I could mask my rage, confusion, and fear with things I could control, like boys and popularity. But moments like this made it difficult. Because I wasn't in control. I was optional.

I hung a few pictures alongside my new trundle bed in Mrs. Bennett's craft room.

It didn't help.

> God doesn't waste our heritage or our home lives. He wants both to shape our true selves.

CHAPTER 7

Dusting Off Daddy Issues

IN A PERFECT WORLD, BABIES ARE BORN TO KIND FATHERS and gracious mothers who are equipped and ready to shepherd their child's tender heart through emotional trauma. Because their parents rightly guided and accepted them, they are now parents who resolve every issue before it does irreparable harm, leaving a legacy of truth-based values and healthy coping skills to their children, grandchildren, and great-grandchildren.

In a perfect world.

We, however, live in a world "groaning with the pains of childbirth," longing to be free of corruption and redeemed to its intended design (Rom. 8:18–22). In our broken world, children often suffer overwhelming attacks to their sense of self and emotional abuses far greater than their parents are equipped to resolve.

I think most of us believe, somewhere down deep, that our parents loved us as well as they knew how. Perhaps you grew up like me, knowing you were loved but rarely feeling wanted

> Maybe you grew up as the object of much affection but never felt truly loved.

or safe. Or maybe you grew up the object of much affection but never felt truly loved.

If you are unsure just how much Annie might be living in you, Dr. Bowlby doesn't leave us hanging.

At the end of his life and research, Dr. Bowlby concluded that our brains are hardwired to ask the same two questions of every relationship we ever have: "Am I safe? Am I loved?"

Dr. Bowlby found that how we answer these questions in regard to the people who raised us determines whether we are able to maintain healthy relationships in our adult lives or tend to sabotage them.

See if any of the following examples from his research resonate with you.

Dr. Bowlby stated that if you felt both safe and loved as a child, if you answer yes to both questions about your childhood, then you are most likely a securely attached adult who:

- Enjoys being around people but also is comfortable being alone.
- Attracts friends easily and maintains friendships long term.
- Enjoys taking risks and going on adventures (trying new hobbies, traveling, tasting different foods, meeting people who are different from you).
- Receives guidance or advice with little offense, readily shaking off a critical word or rejection.
- Holds few to no expectations of people.

If, however, you answer no and yes about your childhood—if you did not feel it was safe to be vulnerable and honest but down deep knew you were loved—you are most likely an adult who is unattached but secure, equipped with enough social awareness to build relationships, but lacking the level of intimacy required to make them last.

Bowlby would describe you as one who:

- Makes friends easily because you are the life of the party and fun to be around.
- Becomes easily depressed or anxious when alone, so you rarely sit still or in silence.
- Often works below your ability and accepts unpleasant tasks to please others.
- Struggles to stay in one place long, always looking for the next, better thing in relationships and work.
- Easily conforms to the behaviors, temperament, and personality of whomever you spend the most time with.

Finally, Bowlby stated that if you answer no and no, if you did not feel safe or loved as a child, you may be an unattached, insecure adult who:

- Struggles to create and keep close friends because you rarely trust anyone.
- Prefers to work in environments in which you are the boss, lead, or are in control of people and positions.
- Is quick to assume the worst of people and often assume that others are talking about you behind your back.
- Is quick to defend your side of the story when confronted with guidance or the possibility of a different scenario.
- Easily writes off a friendship if you get hurt and rarely pursues another for friendship.

If you question God's love for you now, it is only because you have questioned a human's love sometime in your past. Whatever you think of God right now has much to do with what you think about your parents, the first people tasked with loving you and keeping you safe.

If you've ever doubted that your parents loved you as a child, you most likely have spent much of your adult life doubting God's love for you. If you've spent your childhood believing that your thoughts and feelings would be rejected, you may be an adult who struggles with the concept of grace, positioning God as the punisher instead of Jehovah Shalom, the Lord of Peace.

While I pray you are securely attached to loving parents who accepted you more often than they rejected you, my decade as a licensed therapist has shown me how rare the securely attached adult is. Even then, without a parent committed to the hard work of continued self-exploration, the most securely attached among us can experience radical departures from what they know to be true.

Secure or insecure, attached or unattached, we are all shaped by imperfect relationships, by people attempting to love unconditionally from default conditional settings.

The good news is, we are all more the same than different. We all want to belong. We all feel like crap when we're rejected. And we all need the same thing to experience the unconditional love and safety God created us for—one other.

> **The good news is, we are all more the same than different.**

Considering our own attachment style and how we engage our relationships helps us access the only relationship able to fully accept and secure us, a love that needs nothing from us and desires us just because he darn well wants to.

God is our ultimate attachment figure. He is safe and loving, redeeming all unsafe, unloving relationships over the course of our lives to remind us that he is the only one who can always be both safe and loving.

All parents will disappoint us, fail us, and expect too much or too little from us. The love of the most compassionate, present, and attached parent will run out.

But God, being the source and creator of love, is the only relationship with enough reserves to love us unconditionally. And because he has no need for us to love him in return, he will never use our honesty to hurt us.

God will never use our honesty against us.

Taking an inventory of how loved we felt by our parents is healthy and right. Dusting off our mommy or daddy issues heals the wounding of our past in two ways:

1. It gives us a chance to acknowledge what unhealthy habits we are repeating in our adult lives that we once hated in our childhood.

2. It gives us a chance to see our parents from God's perspective. If God seeks to be our ultimate attachment figure, it makes sense that our parents were never equipped to be. This simple reframing ushers in incredible grace and compassion toward the best and worst of parents.

As Paul says to the Philippian Christians, "I have learned in whatever situation I am to be content." But he knows this contentment only because "I know how to be brought low, and I know how to abound" (Phil. 4:11–12 ESV).

To the degree that we've been without is the degree of our gratitude. To the degree we've suffered is the degree of our strength. The lower we've been, the greater our ability to abound.

I wish it hadn't been the "valley of the shadow of death" that finally released the years of resentment I'd harbored toward my mother and father. But I suppose nothing shocks our souls back to life like death.

BABY GIRL BREAKTHROUGH

My mom learned she had multiple myeloma at age forty-eight. Her back broke during a routine chiropractic exam because the cancer cells had already eaten away most of her spine. By the time we caught it, she was stage 4. But the doctors were hopeful that, being young, she would pull through with chemotherapy and a pricey bone-marrow transplant.

By May 2009, we had finally raised enough money to pay for the transplant. Car washes, bake sales, anonymous donations, $65,000 given in total. I knew my mom was beloved in our community, a woman who cheered loudly and smiled brightly for everyone she met. But sitting in that waiting room as she underwent the transplant, I didn't feel a thing.

Everyone around me wept, hugged, and prayed. But I, her own daughter, sat staring at the cover of *Good Housekeeping* for hours, emotionless, numb, cold.

The bone-marrow transplant worked. Deemed cancer free by the doctors by the end of May, Mom squeezed my shoulders and pressed her nose hard into mine once again. "Kasey, we did it. Can you believe they got it? I am going to see my baby girl grow up!"

Baby Girl. Her nickname for Emma Grace, my daughter and her first grandchild.

As much as I hated myself for it, I resented watching her with Emma Grace. My mom said "I love you" to her more in one week than she had to me my entire life. She cried when Emma Grace hugged her, and would cancel her entire day just to watch her toddle around the back yard.

I was thrilled for the gift of Emma Grace during my mom's two-year battle through treatment. Baby Girl was a delightful distraction of youthfulness, energy, and innocence in the midst of disease and darkness. But silently, selfishly, I was jealous, angry that Mom was capable of feelings I had never been chosen enough to see.

There I sat on the seafoam-green sectional in the waiting room, fuming because I was forced to be mom while my mother played, still fumbling through paper sacks filled with cotton gauze and medicine because I was the responsible administering party, still sleeping on a trundle bed in Mom's craft room in case she needed to use the bathroom in the middle of the night.

Three months later, at 8:03 a.m., the morning of Emma Grace's fourth birthday, Mom died.

Despite the initial post-transplant report, the doctors regretfully missed a small shadow lingering in her right lung. This time, the cancer, knowing its way around, made itself at home in every inch of Mom's body. It was a torturous season for us all, but for no one more than for my carwash-dancin', pancake-makin', Great-Lash-wearin' fifty-year-old mother.

As I rushed between spoonfeeding my mom and my new infant son, changing her diapers and his, I found time each day to delicately sandwich Emma Grace between Mom's bone-thin thigh and the hospital-bed railing. I would watch as Mom traced her finger up and down my daughter's porcelain forearm, her chapped lips broken open and blistered from treatment, forcing herself to smile through the pain.

In her final days, Mom's bright green eyes were dark and her voice was lost to a stroke, and I never left her side. Justin brought Emma Grace by the hospital room each afternoon at the same time so Mom could stroke her soft skin and comb her fingers through her lush blonde hair.

Her mind, now in a fog somewhere between our reality and home, began mouthing the same word over and over each time Emma Grace sat next to her—"Kasey."

My grandmother, meeting my eyes across the bed, said, "She thinks she's you, honey."

That night, I clung to the bedsheets at the feet of my dying mother and cried enough tears to fill the blank space of everything unspoken between us.

With Justin sleeping soundly at home with our children, and my siblings sprawled on makeshift chair-beds and wrapped in itchy hospital blankets, I spent the last few hours of Mom's life reminding her of what we both needed more than anything—to belong.

In the end, she belonged to me and I belonged to her. Two strong women capable of loving to the degree of our own acceptance, wounded by those we'd hoped would keep us safe, dismissing our feelings just to get through the next day, and doing our best to raise rebel children through the hurt still healing in our hearts.

With each stroke of Emma Grace's arm, every "I love you" buying back the time, in every one of her final, labored breaths, death did the work it was meant for: it made a way for something new. Like a young girl's body preparing to carry and give birth to a child, pain and blood remind us of God's redemptive design in every moment of our lives.

In Jesus, we "who once were far off have been brought near by the blood of Christ" (Eph. 2:13). In him, we are finally and fully accepted. In him, we belong to a love that makes its home in our hearts, a love that "neither death nor life, nor angels nor rulers, nor things present nor things to come, nor powers, nor height nor depth, nor anything else in all creation" will be able to separate us from (Rom. 8:38–39 ESV).

All these years, the belief that I was unwanted had hardwired itself inside me. Core beliefs such as it is not safe to be honest and feelings are weak simply would not go away after my mom was gone, but there at her bedside in the final moments of her life, I was given a glimpse into the eternal heart of my mother, the reason for her life, the reason for mine.

It was never me she didn't want but herself she struggled to accept. In her childhood she had been left to question whether she was an option. The love of her life, my dad, had rejected her heart one-hundred times over. The guilt and shame of our volatile home life and the divorce forced her to shut down her emotions in order to work a full-time job while caring for her three, hurting children as a single mom. I was not the only one who'd spent the majority of her life questioning her worth. So had she.

In the stillness of the hospital room, I would have given anything for one more whirlwind of cereal boxes, one more makeup tutorial, one more dance around the back yard. I even would have welcomed a Krecia-size blowup over my poor choices in men or one last spin in Trucker Dave's velvet palace.

But when the monitor next to me flatlined, jolting my siblings awake, there was no noise or chaos to soothe us. Only the painful reality that life must now look different. Death would leave a gaping hole, forcing me to choose: dance around it as I'd always done, or for the sake of Baby Girl and those who would come after her, look it straight in its redeemable face.

I could feel all the anger, hurt, and resentment I'd been harboring in my heart for so many years lift from my spirit. So I did what we did—squeezed her shoulders tightly, pressed my nose into hers, and whispered tenderly, "Mom. I love you."

> God does not waste loss but in it inspires us to live for the right things.

CHAPTER 8

Feeling Our Way to God

PEOPLE CAN REINFORCE THE WORST PARTS OF US WITHOUT meaning to or realizing they are doing it.

My mom and dad, for example, loved me the only way they knew how and exactly the way they were loved as children. They had their own stories of heartbreak, shame, and wounding that shaped the barely adult parents they were when I was born. Neither one set out to reinforce rejection in my childhood heart. Neither one of them, blinded by their hunger, could see how seriously starved for affection we all were.

But the chasm between being wanted and being loved in my childhood has significantly shaped who I have been and who I am becoming. Even now as an adult, the fear of rejection can prevent me from fully investing in my family, friends, or dreams. And my actually being rejected can set off one of the biggest chaos storms you've ever seen: a flurry of overbooked schedules, new projects, television binging, and saying yes more often than no.

My fear of rejection said yes to Tanner when he asked to come over, and yes to many "cool cars" after him. The fear of rejection calloused my college-girl heart to the point of sabotaging well-meaning Christian boys who only wanted acceptance themselves. And the fear of rejection set me up to search for belonging in the arms of another man no matter the cost to my marriage or children.

Anytime a child feels that loving them is optional, their heart is wounded. Our desires to be wanted and to be loved are so similar it's difficult to distinguish between them. Not all rejection injuries are traumatic. More often, they are indirect and unintended, making them easier to dismiss, downplay, or deny.

Because childhood injuries aren't easy to see, they often lurk in the heart for years, revealing themselves in adult life.

When I was young, my feeling as though I was optional to my mom triggered a landslide of insecurities that time was not so kind to heal.

Most of us can relate.

Most of us have deep wounds that we never have properly dealt with or processed through the truth of God's Word. Some of those wounds are painful memories, while others have emotionally and spiritually crippled us in areas of our lives.

Rejection is not simply an experience or an emotion, it is also real pain. MRI studies have shown that the area of the brain that is activated when we experience rejection is also activated when we experience bodily pain. Being disliked, offended, or disregarded fires the same network of neurotransmitters.

Neurologically speaking, rejection hurts.

When we cut our leg, we have a visible wound we know needs attention. We douse it with medicine, bandage it up, check it often, and are careful with it until it is healed. We know our leg is ready to get back to work when scar tissue has formed on the cut. Our leg may be tender and it may be some time before we are able to put our full weight on it again, but the wound is closed and the scar reminds us just how capable we are of healing.

But when we are cut by rejection, we can't see the wound, so it often goes unattended, festering and spreading infection throughout our lives, potentially crippling our minds and bodies with diseases like depression and stomach ulcers.

It's an outright lie that time heals all wounds, but it sure does a fine job of distracting us until something painful reminds us that the wound is still there.

> It's an outright lie that time heals all wounds.

THE GREAT FEAR

The sinister thing about rejection, and why we fear it, is that acknowledging it makes us vulnerable. To utter the words "Please love me! Don't leave! I want to be in!" makes us feel weak and fragile. Most of us are taught not to cry over spilled milk, or to get over our tears by pulling ourselves up by the bootstraps, but life just keeps on spilling the darn milk, and for the life of me, I keep breaking the bootstraps.

Rejection is the great fear of humanity because it exposes the truth that we all desperately long for its opposite, acceptance. And the more we consider our desire to belong, the closer we get to the heartbreaking reality that very few people in our lives are able to offer the unqualified love we crave.

When we are loved, we know that someone is choosing to stay in our lives no matter how bad it gets. Safety, however, goes farther. To be safe with someone communicates to our hearts that our bad will not be used against us. A child or an adult may find temporary comfort in another's choice to stay, but if that person stays only out of duty or guilt or to fix us, our greatest fear (rejection) manifests a real belief (I'm not worth it).

As you consider the times you've been rejected, what old wounds resurface?

Our wounds resurface either healed or harmful. But just because a wound is healed doesn't mean it no longer hurts. We may feel sad or cry when we think about times when people have rejected us, but we know the wound is healed when it no longer makes our choices for us.

Unhealed wounds have power over us. They tempt us to question whether God's love is really for us and, because of that, incline us toward behaviors that drive us farther away from his will for our lives.

Because his will for us always reveals itself in one, whole piece, any thought, motive, behavior, or relationship that is working against the other parts is a good indicator that we have a wound that needs attention, and that we are not hearing the Lord clearly.

You can do a quick self-check for undealt-with wounding by running your decisions through the traffic lights of desire, opportunity, and ability. If you get green lights for all three, chances are good that your mind, body, and soul are working in unison to bring you to a healthy, productive, God-willing result.

For example, if you have the opportunity to accept a job that assures you more money, but you don't desire that line of work, it's probably not the best choice. If you have the desire to smoke a pack a day or drink yourself to sleep each night, yet your organs can't maintain health at that capacity, don't do it. If you have the ability to serve on that committee, head up that project, or manage that branch, but the opportunity hasn't presented itself to you, it's best to wait.

God's will for our lives most often presents itself whenever our ability (mind), opportunity (body), and desire (soul) are most integrated. Whenever we chase down one without the others, it's a strong indicator that God seeks to bring healing to an unsettled, unresolved place within us.

If you're breaking out in hives just thinking about all of the possible red lights in your life right now, don't. Remember, you and I are living in God's story. He is not surprised, dismayed, or repulsed by the bad decisions we have made as the result of someone else's bad decisions. He's gone before all of it and has no desire for us to "make straight what he has made crooked" (Eccl. 7:13 ESV).

He wants to clearly show us how he has designed, permitted, and purposed every one of our wounds, as well as those of others, to convince us his will for us is best. And he does that in one specific way.

RIGHT ON THROUGH

As you think back on the most painful people and experiences of your life, you may feel a lot like the apostle Paul did when he wrote, "We felt that we had received the sentence of death" (2 Cor. 1:9 ESV). Now, Paul's life was being threatened; he was in physical peril and pain. But our undealt-with wounds can feel just as perilous and painful.

People who are constantly jabbed with rejection's sharp edge feel like death on the inside. It's why some people (ahem, me) do everything to excess all of the time (overthink, overclarify, overeat, overwork). We need constantly to be doing something on the outside to distract us from the feeling of loss on the inside.

But look at how Paul finishes his statement: "We felt that we had received the sentence of death. But that was to make us rely not on ourselves but on God who raises the dead."

This is God's aim in all of our pain and loss, whether caused by our parents and friends or brought on ourselves. God is using who we are and the people we are surrounded by to knock the props out from under our hearts so that we will fully rely on him.

Whoever you are right now, whatever you're getting right or wrong in relationships, and whether your parents were lovely or unlovely, you are exactly where you are meant to be to receive God's healing.

Acts 1:7 tells us that our times and seasons are fixed by God's authority and that he has "determined allotted periods and the boundaries of their [the nations'] dwelling place." Why? "That they should seek God, and perhaps feel their way toward him and find him" (Acts 17:26, 27 ESV).

Some translations of the Bible use "to grope" instead of "to feel."

I love the image of our groping our way toward God through this beautiful, tragic life. The Greek word used here is *pselaphao*, a verb meaning "to handle, to touch on the surface, to discover through personal investigation, to mentally seek after a person or thing."[3]

This Greek word is also grammatically purposeful: it expresses itself as a point-in-time action, while also being unbound and without time limit. Its placement in the Greek is used not to call attention to itself but instead to draw the audience's attention to the central action of the story.

Part of our "groping" our way toward God is through processing our feelings. Touching, investigating, and mentally seeking why we feel a certain way about what happened is one way to "reach out for him and find him, though he is not far away from any one of us" (Acts 17:27).

The way we feel about a particular experience or person is typically a learned behavior that's been in hibernation. So, what if God orchestrates our lives to happen in such a way that allows us to mentally seek our way to God, ordering all external events to trigger an internal reality he wants us to deal with?

The feelings we experience in a specific event are real and present as a point-in-time action, but from God's perspective, they are also unbound by human time, meant to draw us into the central action of the eternal work God is doing.

Feelings are also unbound by human definition. They are more intricate and complex than can be summed up in any part of our upbringing, race, religious belief, or sexual orientation. But at the same time, they are simple enough to connect all of us in the same way that we all feel anger, anxiety, shame, happiness, disgust, affection, and sadness.

Now, I like talking about my feelings just about as much as I like a low-carb diet. But I adore serving a God who does not dismiss or downplay the most uncomfortable and intricate parts of me.

I love that God wants to acknowledge and talk about the dark, deadly places that sabotage intimacy. I'm so grateful he chose to use every person and place throughout the course of my life to uproot and resurface any feeling that does not rely on him, because I never would choose that course.

I love that, even when we don't have the words to describe what we are feeling or when we struggle to pray, "the Spirit himself intercedes for us with groanings too deep for words" (Rom. 8:26 ESV).

What a mighty God we serve! A loving Father who continually calls us to look back to move forward, to investigate our past until we embrace it as his good and perfect will for our lives.

God is using wherever we are, right this very minute, to draw us to him.

He is using our location on the map, our specific time in history, our biological or adoptive parents, the people who raised us, and whoever our neighbors are to speak to us, setting us up to *feel* our way to him. And yes, because people are complicated and places are always changing, it often feels like we're groping our way to him.

God used a frozen night in East Texas warmed by loads of

uncomfortable questions asked over unending bowls of chips and salsa as the occasion for one attached man to win over the heart of one unattached woman.

Like Justin did for me, the attached people of earth remind us unattached that there is another way, an option for healing and renewal *through* our most honest feelings, not around them. And the unattached remind the attached that the right questions matter. Real people are hurting, displaced, and cast out all around them begging for a relationship in which to share their honest feelings without fear they will be used against them.

The best parents fall short and the worst parents surprise us, and we are all in this together. We all need each other to help feel our way back to God.

Justin will tell you that even on his worst days and throughout his rebellious teen years, he never once doubted that his parents not only loved him but wanted him.

His childhood was not perfect, but his memories are marked by parents who welcomed hard questions, were quick to acknowledge their faults, worked hard to create a routine home in which to receive their children's shortcomings instead of reacting to them, and most important, parented Justin and his sister out of delight, not duty.

Justin says, "My childhood wasn't without hardship, but being loved wasn't hard."

Because Justin's parents set a firm foundation of acceptance, he was rooted enough to offer me one.

Because Justin was never an option to his parents, not loving me after the affair wasn't an option for him.

Because Justin's family valued honesty over comfort, I finally felt safe enough to be honest for myself.

And because God positioned Justin in a strong family, together we could break the generational strongholds in mine, redeeming the lineage of grace through our children.

Before the foundation of the world, God knew I would need a man rooted in security to handle the ice-cold roads I had yet to acknowledge in my heart.

Like me, you may have to kick and scream your way into it, stay ticked off through most of it, show up in costume, brave the cold to get there. However you are feeling your way toward him, don't stop! You are closer than you think.

> God doesn't waste our family histories. He uses them to help us feel our way to him.

CHAPTER 9

Let's Talk about Sex . . . or Not

A FEW MONTHS AFTER JUSTIN AND I WERE MARRIED, WE made the uncomfortable but necessary first visit home to his parents' house as openly sexual partners. Justin, raised in a staunchly conservative Christian home, felt zero stress around the fact that he would be sleeping in his queen-sized, four-post bed with cowboy sheets as a devirginized man. I, however, nervously shifted in my seat at dinner and moved spaghetti around the blue and white china plate. Every plate had an intricate design of a little boy and girl playing ball, running through a field, pulling a wagon. I could have sworn my little girl was judging me from beneath the tomato sauce. "Whore," she said, glaring up at me.

My own sexuality, the act of sex even, had become this terribly shameful thing in my mind. From a childhood full of suppressed memories involving painful male-female interactions to being stuck in the bathroom stall with my "woman's day gift," from my compromising choices with gross, unapologetic boys (not men) over the past five years to my unhealthy Chiquita expose, I was disoriented and confused when it came to God's plan for my body and sex.

It was irrational for me to think that Justin's parents, much less the little girl on my dinner plate, were judging me for parts of me they didn't even know. But the fear of judgment of our past leaves little room for accurate self-perception. This is why it's so difficult for us to remember and deal with the most traumatic, painful memories of our past. So often, we do not live fully alive in the present because our memories still pull energy from us. Without putting words and truth around the experiences of our past, we live in a loop of flashbacks whenever a memory is triggered, experiencing both emotional and physical manifestations of that horrible moment many years later.

> Fear of judgment of our past leaves little room for accurate self-perception.

Not only had I been taught never to talk openly about my feelings, I'd trained myself to manipulate every situation back into my control whenever I feared exposure of those feelings. Because shame's job is to constantly remind us of the worst parts of ourselves, that internal voice in our heads demands that we believe the most irrational, unlikely, fictional version of what other people *might* be thinking of us.

As the night went on, I became even more anxious. My mind could see Justin only as this pure virgin man who'd once dated a soon-to-be nun, and myself only as the girl from the broken family and with the shady past who was here to strip him of the virginity his parents no doubt had worked their entire Baptist lives to instill in him. Although we'd already had sex, in this situation I felt vulnerable and oddly held to account. I'd had little experience of a normal Christian family. I'd had zero understanding, other than what I'd heard at church and read in my Bible, of the freedom one has in married sex. At the core of me, sex equaled shame. Every other message was merely a concept I wished were true of my life. Being completely honest, even Justin made that list. I'd married Justin partly because he looked like the version of myself I one day hoped to be. My marrying him was a bit of a facade that way—our relationship, the goodness of it, was something I wished for in my mind but was still unreal to my heart. I couldn't help but feel like I was wearing a shirt with the word *Jezebel* bedazzled across the chest.

As we all sat around the television sipping coffee, I could hardly stand the tension. Seated next to my father-in-law as he leaned back almost to a sleeping position in his worn green leather recliner, I began to sweat.

The Van Normans enjoyed evenings that ended with old video recordings of *The Gaither Gospel Hour,* a show by a southern gospel group gaining popularity in the 1980s. As "Because He Lives" rang through the living room in five-part harmony, Cheryl began recounting how much she was learning from her new Bible study on worship. I could barely focus on her list of revelations of all the things that we give little thought to but result in an act of worship.

"How we spend our money, the music we listen to, how we speak to people," she explained.

All I could think was, "What if the bed creaks?"

Flushed with embarrassment and ticked off at Justin, who was already asleep on the couch next to me, my words had the pressure of stress behind them.

"Sex! Sex is an act of worship," I blurted, as if to tame the elephant in the room by giving our procreating a spiritual emphasis.

Justin's eyes sprang open as fast as his dad's recliner locked into a sitting position.

Cheryl stared wide-eyed at the television screen as Robert made a sharp coughing noise and Justin slowly covered his eyes with his palm like he had a headache.

No one said a word for the next few minutes. I wanted to melt right there into the embroidered pillows we weren't allowed to lean on.

The only sound was the beginning of the next Gaither song on the set list.

Kill me now, I thought, standing and quickly excusing myself to go to bed. When the first notes sounded, I knew it had to be some supernatural payback for my promiscuous years before meeting Justin. "Goodnight!" I yelled backward, rounding the corner to the bedroom just as the first verse began.

"He touched me, *ohhh* he touched me!"

LITTLE LADY IN WAITING

Sex. The most danced-around, diluted, disreputable topic of my white, conservative, Bible Belt upbringing. I was thirteen years old before I realized that no birds or bees were actually involved in the process, fourteen years old when my body deemed itself procreation-ready, and fifteen years old when forced into a relentless, decade-long obsession with it.

The summer of 1994 served me up a bloom of womanhood with a side of 36Ds. Thanks to my curvy genetic tree, the majority of my freshman class mistook me for a transfer student when I walked through the front doors of Dragon High in my white, Girbaud jeans and new pair of Cole Haan shoes. Who could blame them? The last time they saw me I was three inches shorter, wore braces, had yet to discover an eyelash curler, and could easily be mistaken for a boy with my shaggy, chili-bowl haircut and mosquito-bite boobs.

I was unprepared for the male attention frisking me up and down every hallway and at every locker break. A swap from scoop to crew-neck shirts seemed to help boys find my face more quickly, but there was little to be done to divert attention away from the bloom of my backside.

I'll never forget the first week of library elective when Johnny Peppridge, the most popular guy in the senior class, leaned his chair back on two legs and clamped his fingers on my left butt cheek as I reached to return a book to the top shelf. He held it firmly in his grip and whispered, "Now that's good freshman meat."

I was too shocked and scared to face him. As soon as he let go, I darted to the restroom, hyperventilated, then splashed my face with cold water to slow my breathing. I avoided Johnny Peppridge until the day he graduated.

High school left me dizzy attempting to make sense of all of these children running around in adult bodies wanting adult things.

I, too, and overnight it seemed, felt drawn to the possibility of having sex with creatures that as recently as the previous year had disgusted me. It was the strangest and most vulnerable feeling to wonder whether they also wanted to have sex with me. To feel as though you are on a continual sliding scale of value based on male attention seemed foolish and life-giving all at the same time. To be stared at, groped, whispered about, flirted with, and rated according to cup size see-sawed my heart between what I'd always wanted and what I'd always feared.

I knew the basics of intercourse. Amy Brown's summer sleepover and the eighth-grade sex-education course assured that much. I also knew, as much as it terrified me, that something deep within raced with the desire for it. Whenever Amy giggled, her mouth full of Skittles, through the replay of the night she caught her parents "doing it," I was appallingly mesmerized. The day Johnny grabbed my butt, I was flushed with both fright and flattery.

My confusion about sex stemmed not so much from what I felt but from what I had been taught about what I felt, a conflicting blend of my youth pastor's *True Love Waits* Bible study series and the *Jagged Little Pill* CD by Alanis Morissette I'd confiscated from my brother's secret drawer of unallowables.

Although neither of my parents had been to church since the divorce, I faithfully attended, but only because my grandmother made me and it seemed helpful to grasp at every thread of idealized family I could find. My grandmother picked me up until I could drive myself. Every Wednesday night, without fail, there I sat on the front row of youth group, gripping my worn Bible and frantically taking notes in its margin.

Although my youth pastor preferred goofy stories and long-winded metaphors to teaching through a curriculum, the sudden spike in attendance when Pastor Alex announced his new series on sex could not be denied, sending a wave of deacons on a frantic hunt for more foldout chairs and decision cards.

I never missed a lesson. The following is an excerpt from my journal the last week of the series: "This weekend I get my 'True Love Waits' ring and I am so excited! I wear it on the finger where my wedding ring goes. It will remind me that I don't need to have sex until I am married. Pastor Alex says, 'If a boy tries to have sex with me I can look at my ring and find the strength to say no!' God, I want to stay pure for you. I don't want to have sex. I know sex is a sin before marriage and that when I sin you cannot even look at me. I will never disappoint you. This ring will be my promise to keep myself pure for the man you will give me one day."

As much as an unattached, emotionally wounded, overnight exchange student from pebble to boulder-holder could mean it, I did. At fifteen, on the night of our True Love Waits covenant ceremony, I made a promise to God that I had every intention of keeping.

WITH THIS RING, I DO *NOT*

Pastor Alex must have spent his entire year's ministry budget on that night, moving us down the road to a neighboring church that could better accommodate our numbers and hiring an up-and-coming, all-male praise-and-worship band to perform before the ceremony.

Before signing on the dotted line of purity, we were all invited to "worship" at the feet of this young, gorgeous boy-band with their tan biceps and smoldering eyes gazing back at us through the smoke of the fog machine. A bit "ironic . . . don't you think?"

But as Pastor Alex's voice rang through the auditorium, "Be holy as I am holy!" we shook off our lust coma long enough to walk forward.

All I'd ever wanted was to be wanted. Especially by a man. How could my heart not skip a beat as the pastor foreshadowed the day of our weddings, standing at the altar with us, looking into our eyes and placing small silver rings on our wedding fingers as he tenderly said, "Kasey, with this ring, you commit to honor God with your body, saving yourself in purity until the day you are wed. Do you commit to this covenant with God?"

"I do."

My hand trembled. With tears clouding my vision, I gazed down at the ring shaped as two hands holding a heart with a crown resting on top.

I floated back to my seat, glowing and head held high. I'd never felt more right with the world. Finally, I had a plan to pay God back for whatever had pissed him off in the first place. With purity as the down payment, I could only hope my morality would be enough to compensate for the sins of my family, buying us back into God's good graces.

Pastor Alex never intended to set an entire room of hormone-driven teens up for failure. Like many Christian leaders I've heard over the years, it's not so much what is said but what is not said that has the potential to compromise the message of Jesus.

Our overzealous youth leader spent so much time driving

home the point that God did not want us to have sex before marriage that he never got around to explaining why we wanted to have
sex in the first place. Passages from 1 Corinthians 5 and 6 received
most of the attention: we were to "flee from sexual immorality"
(6:18), we were warned that the sexually immoral will not inherit
the kingdom of God (6:9), and we were "not to associate with sexually immoral people" (5:9). But passages like, "It is not good for the
man to be alone" (Gen. 2:18), "Let him kiss me with the kisses of
his mouth—for your love is more delightful than wine" (Song 1:2),
and, "Let her breasts fill you at all times with delight; be intoxicated always in her love" (Prov. 5:19 ESV) received no airtime.

Driving home after the ceremony, I was still unsure about the
sexual desires awakening within and around me, but I understood
reward and punishment. I could get behind a love to be earned. If
waiting to have sex until I got married was the key to unlocking
God's blessing and restoring some semblance of happiness in my
life, then I was going to be the best virgin anyone had ever seen!
Besides, I wielded the power of the ring, pure kryptonite, as far as I
was concerned, to creeps like Johnny Peppridge. And most important, like Pastor Alex said, I had God's promise to keep me pure.

CROSSING OVER

Although I didn't realize it at the time, growing up in a low-income
neighborhood in a blue-collar family was a great way to keep me
from having sex.

In my hometown you were either rich or poor. Because there
was no local industry, there was only a small group of middle class
citizens. The wealthy and the poor abided by the invisible line
that determined where we shopped, where we worked, where we
socialized, and most important, who we married. My high school

was divided too, split evenly between the jock/prep (rich) students and the grunge/agriculture (poor) students.

The only outliers were freshmen like me who had not yet realized that membership in your class clique was inevitable and necessary for survival. Unless you were lucky enough to land one of the few loopholes. Any rich kid who preferred baggy jeans with a chain to his closet full of Ralph Lauren slacks could cross over, as could the poor kid who wore the same athletic jersey every day hoping to be noticed for his talent, not his economic standing. And so could anyone who had a boyfriend or girlfriend from the other side.

If you landed a boyfriend or girlfriend from the other side, you won yourself a bridge. And if you dated long enough and dramatically enough, you could secure placement on the other side through graduation.

Choir and drama club were neutral territory for class-confused students, the safe zone for anyone and everyone who felt bored by the unspoken rules or was curious about those on the other side. Something about pretending to be someone else, in costume or in song, seemed to erase the line between the rich and the poor.

This is where I met Nathan.

Nathan was an anomaly. A senior jock/prep who was so smart, popular, and talented, he'd done everything there was to do in high school by the time he reached his last semester. In need of an easy class for credit hours, Nathan landed alongside me in drama club just as we were starting rehearsals for our big spring musical.

Nathan was untouchable for a girl like me. I didn't dare approach him or talk to him during class. Besides, he was always surrounded by a posse of prima donnas who could hardly believe they had the pleasure of hosting his final senior months. But that didn't mean a girl from the wrong side of the tracks couldn't daydream. I sat behind Nathan, which gave me a perfect view as our theater director rehearsed lines with the leads. Only a chorus girl myself, still awaiting my dance partner assignment, I had time to fantasize.

Nathan was confident and cute. More like a man than a boy, already accepted to college, the son of a wealthy family with a good Christian reputation.

Most of the other boys showed up for school as if they'd just rolled out of bed—untucked shirt, wrinkled pants, shoes with no laces. But not Nathan. Each day, Nathan dressed for the cover of a George Strait album—starched-collar shirt tucked into a pair of crisply creased Wranglers. My stomach knotted up just looking at him. I gulped hard every time he brushed past me in class, delicately touching my waistline with his hand, smiling, looking straight into my eyes with conviction, "Excuse me, pretty lady." Wink.

Sitting down at my desk, neck breaking out in hives, I would twirl my purity ring round and round my finger, certain that one day I would marry a man just like Nathan.

The rumor was that he and his equally popular girlfriend were each other's "first," but I didn't believe it. I couldn't. Not a godly man-boy like Nathan. He would never compromise a girl's purity. Like he said, I was a lady. And although I was well below Nathan's standard, I believed God wanted to bless me with a husband like Nathan. Every time I caught myself in a daydream, I reminded myself of the prize that awaited me if I could just refrain from having sex. So far, Pastor Alex's charge had been a breeze. Not being attracted to anyone from house grunge and not associating with a Future Farmer of America aided in my chastity.

My plan for success was simple—hide out in drama club until I graduated, go to church, and think about Nathan if I ever felt tempted to date a loser for the sake of crossing over.

In none of my daydreams had I dared to imagine that Nathan himself would become the crossover to beat all crossovers.

A DANCE WITH DESTINY

I just about fainted when our drama teacher called our names together. "Nathan, I'm partnering you with Kasey for the dance number."

Frantically I scanned the room for another Kasey. Casey with a c was somewhere in this school. Her suddenly joining drama club seemed more likely than my being chosen as Nathan's partner. As I sank lower in my seat, Nathan turned around, a cool grin spread across his face and a thumbs-up directed toward the back of the room. I craned around, searching for who he might be gesturing to. Stacey jabbed me in the shoulder. "It's yooou!" she screamed in a whisper.

Look up the word awkward in the dictionary and you will find a picture of me on the day of our first dance rehearsal. I don't think I said a word the entire two hours of step-touch and twirl. Instead, I just giggled and nodded at whatever Nathan said, looking down at my feet, mostly, and sweating so profusely my hand kept slipping out of his palm. The way he smelled, his breath on my neck, the grip of his arm across my back, the sensation of our thighs brushing past one another as we moved—I'd never experienced a feeling like this, all of my senses heightened and engaged at once. I pleaded with the uncontrollable shameful visions to stop popping into my mind, causing me to blush—visions of Nathan yanking me aside into the stage curtain and kissing me like Tom Cruise and Kelly McGillis in *Top Gun*.

I didn't know where those thoughts were coming from. It was the first time I'd ever wanted to be kissed. As weeks of rehearsals and accidental contact flew by, it was the first time I'd ever even considered the possibility of having sex. I felt like a delinquent just thinking about it, distraught that the idea felt so natural to me.

"Does this mean something special?" Nathan looked down at

my ring with his dark brown eyes as he turned it around on my finger.

"Oh . . ." I stammered. "Yeah. Uhmmm, it's a purity ring I got at this church thing."

He chuckled under his breath as he traced his finger over the lines in my palm. My heart raced and I suddenly stopped producing saliva.

"Saving yourself, huh?" he said, raising his eyes to meet mine with a half smile that caused only one of his dimples to form.

"Yeah." I laughed sheepishly, rolling my eyes. "I guess."

As our teacher called the next cue, I shouted inside my head, "You *guess?!*"

I kept asking myself why I'd said that. How could I playfully joke away something so important to me? I felt awful. I didn't mean to offend God. I hoped I hadn't. Things were no better at home: Mom out with a different "dance" partner every weekend, Dad sinking deeper into a depression that only whiskey seemed to treat. I couldn't afford any mistakes that might push God to withdraw his already seemingly limited favor from my life. But as the semester rolled to a close, so did my moral convictions.

I found myself falling for Nathan. Not just in a silly freshman-girl-crush kind of way but in a sincere "stay up at night journaling and begging God to make this man my husband" kind of way.

The day I caught Nathan and his girlfriend fighting outside the theater room, I dared think I might actually have a chance. She glared at me as I walked past. Stacey told me later that they'd been fighting about *me*— Nathan's flirtatious way with me, how he lingered around me after rehearsal, how tightly he seemed to hold onto me even after the dance was over. I'd be lying if I said I hadn't smirked at the thought of her being jealous of someone like me.

Pastor Alex never ventured back into the precarious waters of teaching sex or dating to a room full of humans still growing their prefrontal cortexes and with limited access to their decision-making faculties. But I did stay late after youth group one night to ask him whether God might be preparing a husband for me, even at my young age, to help me keep my purity promise. His response lit a fuse of hope inside me that led me to straighten my shoulders the next time I walked past Nathan's girlfriend and released me to match Nathan's flirtatious advances with my own natural superpower—femininity.

"Yes, Kasey. God knows who you will marry, and he is already preparing him to be a husband to you. You must be patient, trust God, and pray for him to give you strength to save yourself for him. God will bless your purity and lead you to the man who has also saved himself for you."

Sweet Pastor Alex, he did get one thing right. God *would* give me a man who had saved himself for me. But not because of my patience, trust, prayers, or purity.

> God doesn't waste any one of our desires but uses them to help us surrender to our limits.

CHAPTER 10

Life-Defining Moments

AFTER GRADUATION, WEEKS PASSED WITH NO WORD FROM Nathan. On the last day of school, he had slipped me a note that read, "We broke up. I'll call you. Love, Nathan."

Each day, as I babysat my way through summer, I pulled out Nathan's note to reread it, focusing all of my energy on the word love. In my daily quiet time, I scoured the Bible for the word, journaling thoughts on what Nathan most likely meant.

Back then, a neon-pink pager was life. Cell phones were no more than a bulky bag positioned in the console of the car, limited only to parental use. But zings to your hip like 14 ("hi") or 121 ("I need to talk to you one on one") were everything.

There was, of course, the coveted 911 alongside a person's phone number. This meant stop whatever you are doing right now. In the middle of a shower? Get out. Listening to the eulogy at your grandfather's funeral? Leave. Taking a test that will determine whether you pass or fail your class? College is not for everyone. Your friend needs you to meet her in the bathroom right now or she is going to literally die.

The day my hip zinged with Nathan's "911 + number," a wave of heat coursed through my veins and released thousands of butterflies in my stomach. In a few weeks, he would be leaving for college, and he was inviting me to his going-away party. I used every penny of my babysitting earnings to buy a new skirt, wedge sandals, and big hoop earrings to match. I didn't have to beg my mom for permission. It wasn't a date. Just a party with other students, supervised by parents, at the home of one of the most conservative, prominent families in our town. My mom practically hurried me out the door the night of, hoping for herself that I might land an upper-crust crossover.

I drove slowly down Nathan's driveway as I took in the rolling hay pasture and the perfectly manicured crape myrtles and white fencing. Creeping my Buick into park at an ungraceful distance from the house, I started to panic. I didn't see any other cars. Had I come on the wrong day or at the wrong time? That seemed highly unlikely, since I'd memorized and rehearsed every word he'd said over the phone. Just as I shifted into reverse, Nathan appeared in his garage waving me to drive toward him. Sweating through hives and tortured by embarrassment, I pulled my beat-up grandma car closer. I wanted to disappear right there into my ketchup-stained upholstery.

Rolling down the window so as not to seem presumptuous, I cracked out a clumsy, "Sorry! I must have written down the wrong day!"

The same one-dimpled half smile stretched across Nathan's face that I'd seen the day he asked me about my ring. My heart raced and stomach rumbled at the sight of him. He was the most gorgeous thing I'd ever seen. I'd missed him terribly.

"Come inside!" he said, motioning. "You didn't get it wrong." Turning back toward his house, he left me to follow like a lost puppy.

I gathered my keys, pager, and lip gloss, threw them into my purse with a deep breath, and walked through the back door behind him. "Something to drink?" He slung open the fridge door without even a glance toward me.

"No, thanks, I'm good. Where is . . . everybody?"

Slamming the door and popping open a can of soda, Nathan leaned across the countertop toward me. "So . . ." he said, stretching his elbows toward me across the pure granite countertops. "I invited only you." My face turned as red as the can in his hand. "You're the only one I wanted to say goodbye to anyway."

I could hardly believe what I was hearing.

Unless, I frantically rationalized, Nathan is the one. The one God wants me to marry! The thought of it moved my emotions and physical arousal at warp speed. The only shred of this setup that made sense was that Nathan was also in love with me. He must have invited me here to profess that love and ask me to wait for him to finish college so we could be married.

Confidence sparked inside me as I dared look him in the eyes, smile, and respond with a clever, "Oh."

"Do you remember our dance?" he said, swooping me up and pulling me toward him. Every pore of my skin felt like it was on fire as he held me so tight against his body I could barely breathe. His lips brushed against my neck as we swayed slowly through the steps our teacher had beaten into our brains. The faint memory of her raspy yell jolted me from him. "Your parents!"

"Out of town." He snickered, pulling me back in.

Suddenly, I felt like I was going to be sick.

"Hey. I want to show you something." Grabbing my hand, Nathan pulled me to a downstairs bedroom adorned with framed jerseys and custom shelving for trophies. I'd never seen cabinetry made just to hold awards, but there must have been at least a hundred adorning all four walls of his room. In my best attempt to play it cool, I leaned over to peruse a dresser overloaded with framed pictures—Nathan's family, pictures of his tournament teams, and, no surprise, him and his popular girlfriend posed against a themed backdrop for what must have been every school dance since his freshman year.

I replayed this moment a million times over the next five years. It was like watching a scratchy VHS tape: only gray static broken by flashes of images.

That afternoon, on his plaid Ralph Lauren comforter, Nathan raped me. With his elbow pressed into my neck, forearm bearing down on my chest, he was on top of me before I could return the picture I was holding to its chronological position.

"Please, no, Nathan. *Please . . .* stop, *stop!*"

"Shhh . . ." he slithered, over and over again. I'll never forget that sound as long as I live. The sound of a snake.

I stopped squirming when I felt the sharp pain to my groin. Wincing and cramping, I turned my face away from him and squeezed my eyes shut until he finished.

He sat on the edge of his bed staring out his bedroom window and zipping up his starched jeans without a word. I quickly adjusted my new skirt, grabbed my purse, and ran out the back door.

Nathan's driveway, no longer a picturesque cover of *Southern Living*, felt like an overindulgent nuisance. For the first time, I felt proud to be a girl from the other side of town.

"How was the party?" Mom shouted from the recliner as I flew through the door.

"Fine! I just need to use the bathroom." Thankfully, I had my own. A peace offering after the divorce.

I hurriedly wrapped my underwear and my beautiful skirt in toilet paper and threw them in the trash. Feeling the overwhelming urge to be clean, I started a bath.

Drawing my knees up to my bare chest, I watched a trail of bright red blood converge with the pure, clear water. A pink hue spread across the tub, triggering my mind to remember something warm and familiar, like dyeing Easter eggs as a child or sitting in the sink with a scraped knee as my father held me close and washed water over the wound.

I hadn't even had my first kiss. Attempting to understand what had just happened, my brain couldn't provide a definition for a girl who'd had sex without also being kissed. The simplicity and innocence of that thought became my only hope that none of it had really happened, that the entire experience had been nothing but one big nightmare. The ache in my genitals, however, snapped me back to reality.

Just a child, but now every bit a woman, I could have filled my bathtub with the number of tears I cried that night. I cried for all of the obvious reasons. I cried in anger, protest, and sadness. I cried as a victim and as a naive, young girl. I cried as a woman who would face every new relationship believing she was someone's leftovers.

But mostly, I cried because I had never felt more betrayed in my entire life.

Not by Nathan. By God.

All I ever wanted was to make him proud of me, to prove to him that I was worthy of his love and blessing, despite the shambles of my home life. But the dance had changed, and I didn't know these steps.

That night, as I cried myself to sleep, one statement forced itself up through the ice already frosting around my heart: "God, I kept my promise. But you. You did *not* keep yours."

COST-BENEFIT ANALYSIS

It was ten years before I shared the details of my rape with anyone. I spent the months following the incident on a relentless, internal rollercoaster of shame and rage. Now a sophomore in high school, I hid out in the choir room during lunch period to avoid the possibility that my peers might see straight through my skin into the spoiled place within me.

Every day after school, I sped home to quarantine myself in my bedroom and avoid making eye contact with anyone. When my mind raced on replay, I binged and purged boxes of Little Debbie donut sticks and brownies or found reprieve in the authority I had over my own forearm by making it bleed with a tiny prick of my razor blade. While Nathan seemed the better candidate to direct my wrath toward, I rarely thought about him. That is, when I could find one pocket of my hometown where people did not still talk about him.

Nathan had moved on and up, making a name for himself as the newly elected college student-body president. Every other Friday when I visited my mamaw, chances were high I would have to nod and smile as she raved about what a catch Nathan would be for some lucky girl.

Strangely, I could hardly visualize his face when I tried. I could barely make out the words for what I felt toward him. But I was able to articulate very clearly who was to blame for the whole thing. All of my pain, fury, betrayal, fear, and embarrassment made a beeline for God.

"You could have stopped it!" I screamed inside my head on repeat.

"You could have forced my car to break down on the side of the road, slammed his finger in the refrigerator door, made his parents come home early. Something. *Anything!*"

But God hadn't stopped the unthinkable from happening. I couldn't be sure whether he was mad at me or sad for me, or if I'd brought the whole thing on myself. All I knew is that I'd loved God with my whole heart, and for the first time ever, I questioned whether he loved me back.

My entire childhood I questioned whether I was wanted, and now it seemed God had cast his vote too: optional.

At night, staring bitterly at the half-inch-thick layer of dust on my bedside Bible, I would run through scenarios of how I might tell someone what had happened. But after years of watching my mom's talent for doing a rapid-fire, cost-benefit analysis, I'd learned to carefully weigh my options.

Confess my feelings to someone safe, maybe Pastor Alex, and they might respond, "God still loves you!"—benefit.

Further fragment a family that'd already failed the emotional language test and puts hard things under the rug—cost.

Force Nathan to take responsibility and apologize for his wrong because now people know the truth—benefit.

Face the possibility that no one would believe me because it's Nathan's rich, social-elite reputation against my poor, redneck reputation—cost.

People might look at me and treat me differently—cost.

Missing out on a good, Christian man because who would drive a used car when he could buy new?—cost.

Trust God again—cost.

So there it was. The obvious and historically true data convincing my cold and confused heart that honesty was just too risky.

That left me with only one option, an option that life, people, and my church made easy to embrace, a rule handed down to me by generations of hustlers: fake it till you make it.

Or fake it till you break. Whichever comes first.

READY PLAYER ONE

Now that I felt disconnected from my sexuality, I could compartmentalize any emotion attached to it. After months of tears and bleeding in my genitalia, I felt certain that any possibility of future orgasm was now gone as a punishment for the sin of immorality. I had no sensual desire to speak of, no need for gratification.

There was, however, one thing I still wanted. Belonging.

Not unlike every teenager who has ever lived, my life revolved around the desire to be included. It seemed tethered to my soul. I couldn't shake it.

I hated the fact that you needed another person to experience belonging. I didn't want to share my feelings. I didn't want someone to ask a lot of questions or get all mushy and whiny, which eliminated all of my girlfriends. And it was crucial that I be in control.

Keeping my honesty at surface level was the only safe play. I would not risk being hurt again. As long as I said who, what, and how far, I could manage love. Real, fake, who cared? It just had to be on my terms. Besides, I knew this game. I'm talking advanced skill in the art of letting someone get close enough to give you what you need, then pushing them away or sabotaging the relationship once their weaknesses begin to reflect back your own.

I'd watched my dad reserve his affirmation and affection for the days we washed the car without missing a spot or mowed the lawn in perfect three-foot rows. I'd studied a mom who used her emotional-detachment superpower to control relationships and protect her weaknesses.

Thanks to a childhood full of unspoken terms and qualifiers, I knew the conditional-love playbook by heart. All I lacked was a tool for mastering it, something powerful enough to convince someone to choose me on my worst days. Something so detached from my emotions that I would not be tempted to expose or lose control of them. And something transgressive enough that public exposure meant ruin for a teenager growing up in a small town in the Bible Belt.

Like playing a video game on my brother's new Nintendo, I held the controls.

Game of choice: Mortal Combat—High School Edition.

Player: Saint-Slayer Kasey: Church girl by day, sinner by night.
Weapon of choice: Sex.
Ready. Set. Player one?

> God doesn't waste the chaos of life. He uses it to free us from the burden of control.

CHAPTER 11

Honesty's a Buzz Kill

WITH EVERY SEXUAL ENCOUNTER, IT BECAME MORE DIFFI-
cult to discern the difference between God's voice of conviction
and Satan's voice of condemnation. Conviction, healthy guilt drawing our sense of self closer to God. Condemnation, unhealthy guilt
dividing our knowledge of God from the knowledge of ourselves.

There is no compromise like sex to blur the differences
between the voice of God and the voice of Satan. It's the only sin
the Bible says makes one turn on her own self: "Flee from sexual
immorality. Every other sin a person commits is outside the body,
but the sexually immoral person sins against his own body" (1 Cor.
6:18 ESV).

My compromise was always forged in the same place—the
constant pull to be loved, accepted, worth it. I started every
relationship not as a temptress but as a regular girl, a girl just like
your daughter, niece, sister, mom, you.

That's all I ever wanted when I numbed my nerve endings and
shut down my brain for just a few minutes. With every boyfriend,
I hoped the same thing: "Maybe this is the one. Maybe this time
I'll finally . . ."

I started over every semester, like the time I broke up with
Daren Douglas, the guy who let his pet ferret run loose in his

room, and went out with Micah Lowe, the one who showed up out of the blue, interrupting my night shift at the snow-cone stand to say, "Kasey, God told me I should come here. I know we've, like, never talked much, but, my, like, spirit is pointing me to you."

"Who am I to stand in the way of God's will?" I thought.

Turns out, Micah's revelation and promise not to kiss me until our wedding day did not apply to everything else he was "permitted" to do. I felt like Julia Roberts in *Pretty Woman*. "No kissing, it's too personal." But sex, well, Micah taught me just how robotic and detached it can really be, that intimacy does not also require affection.

> One can be intimate without being affectionate.

In every relationship, I couldn't have cared less about the climax. I only ever cared about the feeling you get right before sex messes everything up, the frenzy not of hormones but of possibility.

I felt it while dancing with Nathan before he swept my virginity off its feet. I felt it when I stared weepily into Pastor Alex's eyes the night I received my purity ring. I felt it every time a boyfriend smiled longingly at me or gently held my hand in the school hallway. I felt it at Christmas, the only day of the year my parents tolerated one another long enough to sit in the same room as a family. I felt it in spite of my rage and shame, the possibility that God still wanted me. The still, small voice speaking to my heart, "Kasey, I want you. I choose you. You belong to me."

But that was also the problem. God's voice had become too still, too small for me to hear over my own—or Satan's? I could never be sure.

Sex only ever appealed to me because I could control it. Alcohol, however, was far more complicated. The whole loss of inhibition thing—not my jam.

Both in high school and in college, the notorious experimental years, I was known as the mama bear of the party. I held keys, hair out of the toilet, and the darkest secrets of half the freshman class at my university. I still claim the second stall in the girls bathroom of Nacogdoches Sports Shack club and bar as my first counseling office. Giving advice to drunk girls with mascara-stained cheeks, tequila breath, and sequined miniskirts made me feel important.

Masses of stumbling, slobbering, sick, and already asleep on the ground partygoers would stand (or lie) in line to catch a ride in Camila, my first, real adult car (because it was attached to a real adult-car note). A maroon Toyota Camry with an all-leather interior. She was so fine. And she was the official 1999 Sports Shack carpool for intoxicated persons. Had Uber been a thing in my day, I could have paid my college tuition in one year instead of the thirty it's going to take me.

Announcing to everyone in the room that they'd had enough and that if they wanted a ride, Camila was leaving gave me power, because control was all I needed to get a buzz.

My freshman year, I finally caved to curiosity. I had no intention of getting drunk, but just a buzz would be enough for me to see what all the fake-ID fuss was about.

I simply wanted to know my tolerance, how much was too much for me. Like any good control freak, I planned and coordinated my night of elixir exploration. My friend Cory, the pastor's daughter, was well-versed in the stages of intoxication. I hoped I could trust her to guide me without letting me lose control. So in Cory's apartment, both of us in our pajamas and sworn to secrecy over what was about to unfold, Cory pulled out her stockpile of spirits.

A connoisseur, she presented only the finest for my tasting. A quick tongue tap of each determined that rum was the least wince-producing for me. Moving like a mad scientist in her laboratory, Cory was giddy as she drizzled a bit of this and a bit of that, giggling to herself as she slid her concoction across the table to me.

"You're going to love this. Coke in the bottom. Rum up top. But because the glass is shaped like this," her pointer-fingers outlining the hills and valley of the hourglass-shaped vessel, "when you shoot it back, you'll only taste the Coke, not the Rum. Isn't that so cool?" she cackled.

After the first toss-back, I no longer needed Cory's guidance. She was right! And this was easier than I thought. I could hardly taste the alcohol, and I was surprised by how much I liked the burn setting fire to my esophagus and settling warm into my stomach.

Another. Then another.

Neutrality set in. For the first time in a long time, I didn't care. I very sincerely had no care about anything in the world. I didn't feel sad about my broken family or enraged by my broken body. I didn't care what people thought of me or worry whether I was being good enough for God to bless me. For one, perfect hour of dizzying delight, I laughed and danced and felt as though every sense in my body was born again.

Cory, sliding me shots faster than she could drink them herself, was instantly my best friend. Slobbering and crying over one another, we hugged and apologized and professed our love a thousand times.

About when Cory said "you're my best friend" for the 1200th time, there was a knock at her door. Because everything in the room was spinning, I could barely make out his face when Cory let him in.

Cory opened the door and introduced me to her friend, who apparently lived nearby. "This is my best friend, Kasey. She is sooo beautiful!"

"Yes, she is," he agreed, seeing he'd stumbled into quite a situation.

I threw my forearms across my chest to hide the fact that I wasn't wearing a bra. "Cory! We said no boyzzz!" I sputtered.

"Oh, I'll just stay for a minute," he cut in. "I heard the music and thought I should check on you ladies. Make sure you aren't getting into too much trouble." He winked as he guided me by my arms to find a seat on the nearby sofa.

"Cheers!" Cory bellowed, sloshing him a drink and handing me another, forcing me to unhook my hands from my armpits.

"You know what?" I fake laughed through a sudden wave of nausea. "I'm suddenly not feeling so good. I think I'm just gonna go on to bed."

"Ahhh, I just got here," he moaned and slid closer to me on the sofa.

Nervous, nauseated, and completely annoyed, I stumbled to a standing position and slowly moved toward the bedroom. "Nice to meet you. Really. You kids have fun. Goodnight."

Crashing hard onto Cory's twin bed, I watched the twinkling lights we'd push-pinned across her ceiling dance like fairies in a circle. I'd never felt so tired. My body felt a hundred pounds heavier than normal. Fully dressed, I wanted to at least rid myself of my socks and burrow beneath the covers, but I had not the energy to lift, bend, or toss a single thing. Finally, I succumbed to the darkness. (That's a pretty way of saying I passed out.)

The next day, I awoke to a Mack truck running over my head and torso. I slowly lifted my head enough to catch a view of Cory's wall clock through the haze of crusted-on masacara: 1:00 p.m., it flashed in red.

I catapulted to a sitting position. "How is it 1:00?! My boss is going to kill me!" I thought. I wailed, crashing back down onto the bed.

Death itself could not hold a candle to what I felt. Not only did I still feel drunk, I was most likely going to lose my third part-time job cleaning beds at the tanning salon. Every muscle, joint, and nerve ending in my body felt as though they were being tortured by my breathing. I tried to hold my breath to stop the spinning for a second. But then, forced to exhale, I got a whiff of the terrible smell coming from my mouth, which sent a chill down my spine and a rush of vertigo to my head.

Cory may have been my best friend, but rum hated me.

Holding my body as still as possible, freezing my neck as though in a vice, I raced my fingers across my shoulders, breasts, stomach, thighs in confusion. I strained to think.

Why was I naked? I pursed my lips and exhaled slowly as if through a straw.

Beginning to panic, heart rate elevating, I felt with my hands for my underwear, bra, pajamas, the socks I hadn't had the energy to take off. They were not on me or anywhere around me.

Cory was nowhere to be seen. I yelled an excruciating hoarse "Cor!"—hack, cough—"Cory!" More hacking and coughing.

I had to get up. With every ounce of my will, pulsating with regret and confusion, I commanded my body out of bed. The rush of blood to my brain sent a wave of dizziness over me, buckling my knees and forcing me to grasp a nearby desk chair.

Grabbing the towel Cory'd wrapped her wet hair in the night before, I swaddled my naked body and walked slowly toward the bathroom. With stomach acid bubbling its way toward the top, I knew my date with porcelain was inevitable, so I picked up the pace. Cory was sprawled on her living room sofa where I'd left her, still wearing her pajamas. In the bathroom, I wept and groaned through two solid hours of heaving that rivaled a grown man's deadlift competition.

In those brief seconds of pure relief and hope at the end of each retch, I sipped water from the sink faucet and lay in the cold bathtub, shaking, drawing up a few damp bath towels and loofahs to support my neck. Just when I thought it safe to stand, one more surge of reflux propelled me up and over for another retch, then another.

Cheek pressed against the brim of the toilet bowl, lying in my own excrement, tears dripping into the toxic water below, I stared callously at the used condom that had been thrown into the trash can next to me. I'd noticed it somewhere about round three of twenty-three. Slowly and with much labor, I deduced the most likely scenario.

Cory, finally rousing from her stupor around 5:00 p.m., confirmed my suspicion. She remembered drinking and talking with her neighbor for nearly an hour after I'd gone to bed, and then shutting and locking the door after his exit, but that was about it. The pockets of her memory I needed were gone.

As I quietly cleaned up after myself, Cory kept rounding the corner to apologize and to repeat how uncharacteristic this was of him. I just let her talk and bring me another cracker, mainly because I couldn't find the strength to tell her to shut up.

She felt horrible about letting this guy come over, but I just felt numb.

> God doesn't waste the reckless days of our youth. He uses them to shape our redemption.

CHAPTER 12

Listening to the Right Voice

I HAD NEVER BEEN MORE NERVOUS. SITTING TO MY RIGHT, A volunteer college freshman who needed extra credit. To my left, behind a one-way sheet of glass, the entire faculty of my graduate counseling department. The next thirty minutes would determine whether I would be deemed worthy of a license that would set me loose on the world to help people with their problems.

Three years of sleepless nights, study, and many tears all boiled down to this one, career-defining moment between me and an acne-ridden, fidgety young man who gripped his backpack tightly in his lap and preferred not to shake my hand. This was my final exam: to effectively use my learned counseling techniques to serve this pretend client with his very real problems.

I knew the techniques: leading questions, redirections, healthy transitional statements. I knew all the right words: "So you're saying that . . ." "May I say that back to you?" "Thank you for trusting me with this information." I'd read and reread my "client's" background file prior to our session. Before he walked through the door, I knew his presenting problem was anxiety and that he wanted help dealing with his pornography addiction. (Of *course* I would draw *this* guy's name at random.)

But when this poor guinea pig sat eyeball to eyeball with me,

135

none of what *I* knew mattered. Where he was, who he saw himself to be, and what he wanted to do about it—these were the only facts that mattered.

I could guide him, encourage him, reframe, ask new questions, and offer healthy alternatives, but I could not take ownership of his problems or the solutions to them. Offering him the *what* without his first identifying his *why* was no more helpful than offering him a Xanax or passing him another *Playboy*.

Thirty minutes with an inexperienced counselor like myself would not even begin to come close to uprooting why this young man used anxiety and pornography to reinforce the thing he wanted to avoid. But it would be enough to teach this green therapist, herself in need of therapy, a life-altering lesson: you can't *should* on sin.

LEADING QUESTIONS

Sin, our choice not to trust God, will never change into a desire to trust him as long as we are listening to all of the other voices telling us who we should be, how we should live, or what we should do.

Rules, rituals, religion, tradition, and the opinions of others have only enough power to change us at a surface level. They may help us exchange unhealthy behaviors for socially acceptable ones, but we will have no peace until we choose for ourselves to obey God.

For example, we may exchange our smoking habit for the more socially acceptable indulgence of eating pastry. Or release our energy through working out instead of through masturbation. But even though our *what* has changed, our *why* has stayed the same.

Why does anyone need a high of any sort—nicotine, sugar, adrenaline, sexual release? Because God has not become so real to their hearts that he satisfies them.

God knows what onlookers do not: our hearts. "For the LORD

sees not as man sees: man looks on the outward appearance, but the LORD looks on the heart" (1 Sam. 16:7 ESV).

God knows the pocket within each of us that holds everything that's happened to us. He sees the whole story, the reason why we do what we do. He knows how stuck we feel, how numb, paralyzed, or cold we've become because of all of the pain and regret inside our hurt pockets.

God also knows that his truth will not become real to us as long as we are exchanging behaviors. That's why he doesn't get his feathers ruffled by our displays of sin. He knows what humans struggle with most, that once our reality rests in him, our sinful behaviors will work themselves out on their own.

God doesn't want us to repent of our sin because we think we should. He wants us to own it, a decision that we make for ourselves not because we think we have to but because we want to.

Just look at every event and person in your life as a leading question, not as a demand. Like when Jesus says to his disciples, "I know what others say. But who do you say that I am?" (Matt. 16:15).

Consider every high and low you are fumbling with in that hurt pocket of yours as an opportunity for God to ask you a question. "When your father abandons you, who do you say that I am? When your wife betrays you, who do you say that I am? As you wait through infertility, singleness, chronic back pain, or mental illness, who do you say that I am?"

Life is one big, leading question with God as the answer.

Even Satan knew better than to tell Eve what she should do.

Telling her to eat the fruit would not be personal enough to change her from the inside. It may have been dramatic enough to change her mind or feelings, but only through reasoning inside her life would Eve form a new belief that would change herself and the world around her.

So like any good counselor, the serpent started by asking her a simple question.

"Did God actually say, 'You shall not eat of any tree in the garden'?" (Gen. 3:1 ESV).

WHO TOLD YOU THAT YOU WERE NAKED?

Much like God, the enemy also is not satisfied with a few shifts in our behavior. He wants his lie to become our truth, a real belief that manifests in our identity and changes our behavior from there.

But unlike God's, Satan's voice is not powerful enough to speak directly to our hearts. He is not tied to our DNA or woven into our image. He is left only to formulate leading questions. And his questions are designed to confuse and disorient us, to isolate us long enough that our reality feels blurry, fragmented, and compartmentalized.

> Unlike God's, Satan's voice is not powerful enough to speak directly to our hearts.

Satan can speak only to our *what*, the external pieces of our lives—words and actions, what we do and say. But God will always speak to our *why*—our hearts, motives, beliefs, desires, wants.

A created being himself, Satan is allowed only enough power to point out our vulnerabilities from what he observes about us. But God is the one who determines whether those vulnerabilities make us acceptable or unacceptable to him.

Unlike Satan, who has access to us only through our behaviors, when God speaks, his words are attached to our hearts: "Living and active, sharper than any two-edged sword, piercing to the division of soul and of spirit, of joints and of marrow, and discerning the thoughts and intentions of the heart" (Heb. 4:12 ESV).

When God speaks, our hearts cannot help but be nagged, drawn, intrigued, or compelled to attention. For only God speaks with the authority of eternity to the whole picture of our past, present, and future as it matters to heaven.

"He said, 'Who told you that you were naked?'" (Gen. 3:11).

> Only God speaks with the authority of eternity to the whole picture of our past, present, and future as it matters to heaven.

"Look around, Adam, Eve. Just a few moments ago, you were naked and unashamed. Now you're sewing fig leaves together to cover what I deemed good. Just a few moments ago, you were standing upright in the light of day, basking in the beauty of provision that was yours for the taking. Now you're hiding out in the dark. Why? Whose voice are you listening to?"

Notice God's question lifts the burden of earning love by pointing to the one who assigns love's value in the first place: "Who told you?"

But Satan's question adds a burden by pointing to the possibility that Eve may have heard wrong and therefore is deficient in some way: "Did God really say?"

In the Bible, nakedness means you are known all the way down to the deepest part of your vulnerability and weakness. When we are living in honesty before others, we no longer feel the urge to control the information they receive about us. We don't need fig leaves, a garden, a master control, or a game plan. When belonging to God is our reality, there is no more need to run, hide, blame, or mask our feelings with drunkenness, revenge, isolation, or manipulation.

Adam and Eve didn't lose their clothes, because they never had any to begin with. But they did lose something precious—they lost their purity, their innocence. They lost their ability to stand unashamedly before their maker.

Voices are speaking to us even now. One voice whispers a lie that divides our humanity and separates us from others. The other speaks a truth that makes us wholly known and eternally accepted. And while the voices' message differs, they both speak the loudest in our pain. We are never more keenly aware of the voices speaking to us than in our weakest moments: when we need, when we lose control, when we fall short of someone's expectations, when we stand in front of a mirror and view our aging, sagging, frail, mortal bodies.

Some of us will use a leaf-sewing needle until our fingertips bleed before we let ourselves out of hiding. Others will spend a lifetime going round and round in a heady, theological debate with the serpent, countering every one of his questions with another one of our own, always needing the last word, never quieting down long enough to hear there's been another voice speaking all along.

At the end of the day, when we lay our heads down on our pillows, when our honest thoughts are "naked and exposed to the eyes of him to whom we must give account" (Heb. 4:13 ESV), whose voice speaks to us?

I don't know what heartache you might feel when you read these words, but God loves you so very much. So much he sent himself to you not to condemn you but to save you.

Jesus' light ruins us for things that live in the dark, the highs that never satisfy our inmost being. Because the light has come into the world, the darkest night of our souls can be exposed for what it truly is: not God.

Whether or not we realize it, we all want to come to the light. We want ourselves and everyone around us to live transparently wherever we are on the road of working out our salvation with fear and trembling (Phil. 2:12).

At our core, we know that only in the place of honesty will our purity be restored, that only in our willingness to bring forward, look at, and understand the most painful, disgusting, and difficult things about us will we find the freedom to stand before God and others unashamed.

The more often we choose to listen to the voice of God, the more convinced we will become that God sees our weaknesses dif-

> Only in honesty will our purity be restored.

ferently than we do. Not as embarrassing moments we need to dismiss or dilute with drunkenness but as useable material. What seem like scraps to us are God's best resources to prove his love for us once and for all.

For God's purpose to be clear in our lives, we must get honest with ourselves about our darkest days, the days we want a buzz, need to numb, continue to do the thing we hate. Honesty acknowledges that there is both a victim and an offender within us, that "none is righteous, no, not one" (Rom. 3:10 ESV).

We are all exposed before God, but who is telling you that?

You don't have to be as hardheaded and stubborn as me to believe the voice of truth. Twenty years as a Christian, believing in God, but never believing him.

No more still, small voice for me. God was about to drop the mic on my wimpy, lukewarm faith. The fake me was about to get the buzz kill of her life.

And when she did, there'd be no doubt, for her or anyone else, whose voice was speaking.

God doesn't waste our worst days. He uses them to tell us the truth.

CHAPTER 13

It's All Just One, Big Setup

WE'D BEEN ASLEEP AS HUSBAND AND WIFE NOT EVEN TWO hours when Justin belted out, "Well, *look*-ey there!"

Jolting from dead sleep and catapulting upright, I fumbled with the bedsheets and clumsily searched for a light in our dark, unfamiliar honeymoon cabin.

"Wha . . . whaaat's wrong? What is it? Who's there?" I said groggily into the darkness.

It took a few seconds to remember where I was and who I was sleeping next to. I tumbled hard onto the floor from the tall, cedar-framed bed, comforter wrapped around me like a cocoon, where with only the clock light to guide me, I fumbled around.

Justin broke out in mischievous laughter, prompting me to move faster.

Belly crawling across the floor, I finally felt the cord to a lamp. Wrestling the lamp to the floor beside me, tossing the shade aside, and turning it on, I could finally see what I was supposed to be "lookey-ing" at.

Pointing through an open cabin window into the eerily dark mountains that surrounded us was one very hairy, very naked man—my new husband.

"What?" I screamed. "*What is it?!*" Pulling what covering was left from the mattress, I wadded them up to create a protective barrier against whatever was about to come through that window.

Waves. White sand. Loud music. Sunburn. A hint of coconut in the air. I'd been dropping these honeymoon hints for months. But I soon learned that my new husband had zero knack for subtlety or context clues. He couldn't take a hint if you handed it to him on a plate. The one thing I'd asked Justin to do, his only responsibility in six months of wedding planning, was to locate and book the perfect honeymoon spot. And here we were, on our first night as husband and wife, about to make headline news: "Naked Newlyweds Found Mangled by Moose." Or "Barely Wed Make for Great Bear Bed."

Because one can hardly see straight in the dizzying, smitten frenzy that is engagement, I'd spent the six months prior to our wedding fake smiling and nodding while Justin proudly boasted over his chosen honeymoon destination—Estes Park, Colorado.

A majestic spot, truly.

Great place to ski in winter.

We were married in May.

Boutique shop and wine tastings in all seven available establishments.

We were very broke and very Baptist.

Fabulous place for hiking, sightseeing, and birdwatching.

Not on the to-do list of this twenty-two-year-old newlywed who'd worked three jobs in order to singlehandedly plan and pay for her entire wedding.

I'll give him some credit. He did spring for the cabin with the heart-shaped hot tub inside. But the owners forgot to turn on the warmer before our arrival (it being May and all), so the water never rose above lukewarm. It was a nice, first bath together. Shivering in our swimsuits. The sparkling cider wasn't enough to warm us up.

Although I couldn't bear to tell Justin, all I really wanted to do on our weeklong honeymoon was sleep. Well, that and, you know. But that was it! And that second part mainly because, poor guy, it's just . . . he'd been waiting his whole life to *do* it. I felt like I was a benefactor handing over a multimillion-dollar estate that would change his life forever.

The sex we'd not had throughout two years of dating surprised no one more than me. Shockingly, my controlling a man's commitment to me through sexual advances never once derailed me with Justin. But only because he stopped things before they started. His ability to pull away from my embrace at the exact moment most boys flipped the switch of compromise intrigued me, kept me on the hook. *Hmmm. What's wrong with this guy? I should stay long enough to find out.*

But after a few manic episodes of insecurity—slamming doors, stomping away from an argument I'd started, pouting through a movie because I'd felt rejected or ugly—our relationship settled into a love unlike any I'd ever known. A true one.

Over time, his secure, peaceful presence broke me down. Justin did not respond to my flirtatious advances or passionate sermonettes on how I needed him to pity my wounded heart. I gave it my best attempts, used every feminine ploy and manipulation tactic in my arsenal, cried, whined about my daddy issues, moved my hand a little lower. I think at one point I even begged. Not for sex, specifically. Just for more. More of what, I didn't know. More affection, I suppose, time, empathy, comfort. I always wanted him to work harder to fill the voids inside me.

I thought I would break him. Instead, Justin's patient, calm, humble manner kept drawing me in and wearing down my edges. With few words and no emotion to speak of, he tempered me, taught me. Tenderly grabbing my hand back or holding my gaze in silence until I finished my rampage, Justin showed me another way, a love that could long and desire and hope not from a place of deficiency but from a place of overflow. A love strengthened by reserves from years of consistent handling.

Justin didn't need affirmation or praise. He didn't care for gifts. And although he constantly reminded me how physically attracted he was to me, he never used that attraction to satisfy unmet desire within himself. I couldn't even get a good argument or debate out of him. Like talking to a one-way mirror was squabbling with this guy. He'd just stand there stoically following me with his eyes until I shut up or walked out.

Throughout our dating relationship, Justin consistently told me how much he treasured me, how valuable and precious I was to him. And now the day was here. We were an official and blessed union. Free to consummate at will and at pleasure. Justin could finally unwrap his treasure.

And I felt like I was giving him a gift. Yes, in a heartfelt "even still, you blessed me, God" kind of way. But also, in a weird, proud-mom, "you did so good staying a virgin, honey!" and "I'm going to rock his world" kind of way.

Here I was, finally having sex the way I'd always wanted and with the man of my dreams. Who, as it turned out, was also in a dream. The man who'd saved himself for me also held out on the confession that he talked and walked in his sleep.

There stood my prince in all of his "no longer a virgin" glory, with his naked pasty-white butt, hollering and pointing out an open window in the middle of the Rocky Mountain National Park, where the daily, afternoon descent of bighorn sheep seemed more interesting to him than the 36DDs tumbling out of the swanky lingerie I'd toted along.

As Justin walked back to bed, fully asleep and with a sheepish grin on his face, I clenched the cotton sheets tighter to my chest, mouth open wide and still unsure exactly what I was looking at. Justin laid back down, completely still, totally unclothed, coverless and not at all shivering in the frigid mountain air gusting through the window he'd opened and knocked the screen out of.

Seconds passed. Stunned and speechless, I wondered if it was safe to approach.

"Justin?" I whispered shakily, reaching my hand toward his shoulder. As I did, my armorless knight bellowed one more REM battle cry, causing me to stumble backward into the lamp, trip over the cord, and fall to the floor.

"Circle the wagons, boys! Circle the wagons!" he cried, never once waking.

After quietly shutting the window and gently covering Justin with a blanket, I thought it best to spend the rest of my night contemplating my new life right where I landed—the floor. After almost an hour of mind-racing questions and possible regret, I drifted off to a line from one of my favorite movies. "Congratulations, Kasey," I thought. "This is all just a real nice surprise."

A REAL SURPRISE

In an iconic scene from *National Lampoon's Christmas Vacation*, cousins Clark and Eddie are walking through a store shopping for Christmas when Clark realizes that Eddie doesn't have enough money to buy presents for his own children. Clark, desperate to salvage some piece of his epically failed Christmas plans, offers to help out. "This isn't charity, it's family," Clark says proudly.

Eddie responds with a bear hug for Clark, and whips out a long, specific, and alphabetically organized Christmas list for his entire family. "Well, this is just a real nice surprise," Eddie repeats over and over again, pounding Clark on the shoulder as he hands him the list. "And if it wouldn't be too much, Clark, I'd like to get something for you. Something [wink] real nice." Clark is stunned.

Something like this happens, many times over, in marriage. One person offers to give of themselves for the benefit of the other. At first, the gesture is sincere. No one resents the other for taking half the closet space or begrudgingly shares the bed because the other talks, snores, or tumbles about in their sleep. And she never curses him in the middle of the night when her butt cheeks hit water because he left the toilet seat raised.

For the first few years of marriage, self-sacrifice is not charity, it's family.

Because you are a team, you feel stronger and more confident and are generous with your time, energy, and passion. Offenses are quickly forgiven, and differences chalked up to the endearing attributes that balance you with the other.

In the beginning, you are both sincere, willing to compensate for one another's deficits. You even feel all warm and proud inside when you see your spouse's face light up because of something you've done to help them feel a little more seen and understood in this big, crazy world.

But after a few years, their list of needs just seems to be getting longer, while yours goes mostly unfulfilled. You're a bit shocked, perhaps appalled, that your spouse continues to ask anything of you, because you can't remember the last time they sacrificed anything for you.

Looking at your own list of needs, you think, "Are we still a team? Am I really supposed to spend the rest of my life with this person? What if nothing ever changes? Is it worth it?"

Maybe he's hairier than you thought or never warned you that he reenacts old westerns in his sleep. Maybe you wanted the beach but got mountains instead. Perhaps even glimmers of hope, like the heart-shaped hot tub, have turned out to be nothing but lukewarm bathwater. Maybe you're married, or really want to be, but find yourself mostly dazed and confused, fumbling around in the dark, desperate to find just one ray of light.

Whether we are single, married, divorced, betrayed, or beloved, life is just one, big, ever-evolving surprise, not always nice or mean. Sometimes a small turn of events knocks us off center (or in my case, off the bed) to think it through for a night. Other times, surprises slam into us so hard, they redirect the course of our lives.

Never forget, life is just one, big setup!

We easily get caught up daydreaming about the finale. We want to know the final scene of our stories. So instead of enjoying the moment, we let our minds drift toward all the things we have yet to do, the person we have yet to become. We compare and bemoan our lot in life instead of enjoying the provision and favor given to us right where we stand.

When we catch ourselves easily dreaming and drafting a better scenario for our lives than the simple, self-sacrificing one God has called us to, God is good and right to remind us that his will works no matter how much we whine.

This universe is God's train. And his train is moving down the tracks whether or not we like it or want to be on it.

His will for our lives will work, no matter how much we whine.

God has every right to abandon us when we forget his faithfulness. But in his mercy, he disciplines us instead, to bring us back to himself, to use all of his divine power and resources to shock, stun, traumatize us, if necessary, back into the reality that his love is the only love we are designed to trust completely.

God knows that the closer we are to him, the closer we are to who we are meant to be. He proves this over and over inside our stories, in our ever-changing scenes and settings, with all of our heroes and villains, through our comedic blunders, and in our climactic events.

Like guiding millions of Israelites on a forty-year trek in a wilderness that should have taken eleven days, God rightly knows what we so often question. His process is the point. The journey toward the promise is the only thing that will give us the courage to claim that promise in the end.

For us to fully believe who we are in God, right here in this moment, based not on what he does but instead on who he is, life on our terms must come crashing to the ground.

All the spinning plates of busyness we've collected over the years must fall. The buzz of distraction and comparison must be sobered. We must bring all of our secrets into the light, expose our sacred snapshots, dust off all of our mommy and daddy issues so that we might actually feel for once. Maybe we tumble down the mountain of our pride or face-plant so hard that we're out for years. Maybe we need to go back to church or spend some time in prison. We most definitely need to put sex on the table and call it what it is, confessing all of the uncomfortable, awkward, unlikely ways God has faithfully used to set us up to know he is exactly who he says he is.

His process is the point.

BARBIE CAR INSURGENCE

When Emma Grace was four years old, she loved puttering around our yard in her hot pink, Barbie Power Wheels. I say yard, but we built our first home atop a hill in the middle of a picturesque, ten-acre Texas hay meadow. Needless to say, the girl had plenty of room to ride. It could've been ten thousand acres for all she knew.

I designed our home with a massive kitchen window that allowed me a 180-degree view. I'd position my laptop at the table right where I could glance over and see Emma Grace peddling around outside. A white fence bordered our property on all sides, and a gravel drive wound down to our entrance to the red-dirt access road. And since we really lived in the country, we had no use for gates. We kept our house unlocked and left our keys in the ignition most of the time.

On the other side of the entrance, where our white fence opened, the access road turned sharply, making it almost impossible to see oncoming traffic. You had to position yourself just right to get a clear view of approaching speeding cars (no speed limit signs in the real country) or slow-moving tractors.

Each day before Em ventured out, I leaned down, pushed her thick blonde bob back from her face, looked into her eyes, and said, "Remember, love, you must stay inside the fence. See all of this? [*waving my hand in the air toward the Bermuda grass now several inches taller than her*] You can ride your jeep anywhere inside here, but you must not go outside the gate to the road where the cars cannot see you." She'd bobble her head up and down with excitement.

Emma Grace was compliant for months of play. But one day, I noticed her lingering closer to the entrance. Day after day, she parked her little Barbie Jeep, climbed out, took a few steps toward the road, and just stared. Sometimes I noticed her talking to herself or picking up a stick and motioning to her dolls in the passenger seat. I could see her tiny lips moving fast and serious, warning her friends about all sorts of things, about the dangers that lay beyond the "kingdom's wall," perhaps.

She was getting curious about the road. I would stand on the front porch, only a quick sprint away, and watch her think it through, every now and then looking back to see if I was watching. I'd most often just let her be curious for a while. If I felt even a nudge of uneasiness, all I needed to do was yell, "Emma Grace!" in a sharp tone, and she would quickly turn, jump back into her Jeep, and putter slowly back to me.

She ventured closer every day. Then one time, the look on her face changed, and I knew she was ready to rebel.

Sure enough, her mismatched romper and boots planted themselves in her Jeep alongside her favorite stuffed animal, Glue Kitty (tragic story involving a hot glue gun and wild boar goes here), and set off toward the opening in our fence. I knew she was determined when I saw those cherubic cheeks look back at me with every jolt from the uneven gravel beneath her plastic tires. I also knew it would take her forty-five minutes to make it three feet. So I had time to think this through.

I could rush out the door screaming and scolding, "Emma Grace! What do you think you're doing? Get back here right now, you're going to kill yourself!" But that would just scare her. A small memory at best, but perhaps traumatizing enough to register in her baby brain as "curiosity, bad; Mommy, mad."

I could, without a word, walk out and yank her from her seat, squeezing those chunky arms tighter with each fit of protest or limp body drop. Once we reached the house, I could drag her into her bedroom with a "Sit in here and think about what you've done. You better mind me next time, Miss Priss." But nothing would be solved and she would resent me. Putting her in time-out would address only her behavior, not her heart. As I knew well from my own childhood, time-outs offer little more than the opportunity to craft a better plan for the next revolt.

We could rethink our open fence, add a gate to protect her. But wouldn't that just increase the mystery of the road? Besides, one day, she'd be old enough to drive a real car out of the fence any time she pleased, making her own decisions about what was safe or perilous.

But I couldn't just let her toddle into the road.

What was the most loving mommy-move?

Without running or screaming, I slowly walked toward her as she continued her labored trek. She paused, noticing me. I smiled warmly, signaling that my presence meant no harm or punishment. She continued.

I positioned myself in just the right spot. Closer, closer. Emma Grace, now only ten to twelve feet from the road.

Just then I heard a spitty tractor engine. From where I stood, I could see our neighbor, Tom, beginning his daily afternoon outing to feed cows. His vintage tractor moved about as fast as Emma Grace's Barbie Jeep.

I could not have set the scene better if I tried.

Emma Grace could have been planted in the middle of the road and dear, old Mr. Tom, going as slowly as he was, still could have stopped twenty feet from her. His beast of a tractor also took up the entire one-way road, so there was no chance of a car getting around him until he had a mind to let them. But Mr. Tom never had to make that choice. Emma Grace stopped just short of his loud, ornery machine.

As the giant, oversized tires rolled past her, a wave of surprise and fear quickly melted her childish ambitions. The reality of the road catapulted her out of her toy car and into my arms. As she trembled and teared up just a bit, I knelt to hold her. "It's okay, honey. You're safe. One day, when you're old enough, you can go on the road too. But for now, please trust Mommy when I ask you to stay in the fence."

If he wanted, God could just stop us from doing something stupid. He's strong enough, wise enough, and able to see the road we cannot. He could simply take away all of our fun, scold us, put us in time-out, or put up a gate to imprison us inside his will. But God doesn't want us to simply believe *in* him, he wants us to *believe* him, to trust that his way really is the best way and that when he asks us to obey him, he does so only from love and always for our good.

"If you then, who are evil, know how to give good gifts to your children, how much more will your Father who is in heaven give good things to those who ask him!" (Matt. 7:11 ESV).

> God doesn't want us to simply believe *in* him, he wants us to *believe* him.

Emma Grace never tested her boundaries again, because she didn't need to.

Even as a child, she could see that her way led to harm, while my way offered just as much adventure, but from the security of home.

I never would have allowed her to be crushed, but I did want her to feel the wind of death long enough to believe me.

Sweet girl, I loved her enough to set her up never to doubt my love for her again.

> God doesn't waste our rebellion. He uses it to set up real faith.

CHAPTER 14

When Nothing and
Everything Changes

NOTHING AND EVERYTHING HAD CHANGED FOR US SINCE
meeting Rachel and Ty.

Big, wonderful moments, like the birth of our first child,
bonded Rachel and me even more. Born only three weeks apart,
their son and Emma Grace were the best of baby friends, wincing
through smashed peas, cutting their first tooth, and taking their
first steps together.

Our families had never felt more connected. We were all doing
our best to balance work, sleep, responsibilities, and keeping an
entire human alive.

Rachel and I would talk on the phone for hours during the day
while the menfolk went to the office. Sometimes, we would just put
the phone on speaker while cooking, taking a shower, or running
errands. Rachel and I were truly one another's lifeline.

We connected to each other on just about everything, except
one big thing—our feelings.

While Rachel felt perky and ready to take on the day after only
four hours of sleep, I would have given my left breast for just one
more hour, pondering at length whether it was possible to establish

an intravenous drip of coffee. While Rachel never seemed sad or scared in her new role as mom, I felt both all of the time, much more often than I confessed to her.

It was the first time in our friendship I'd held something back.

I trusted her with just about every secret from my past, but I was too ashamed to trust her with the truth that she and I were two very different people.

Like Justin, Rachel had never gone a day in her life questioning whether she was wanted. An only child, born into an affluent family, Rachel married straight from her father's loving arms into Ty's. While she attentively and graciously listened through the years of tears of my backstory, she never fully grasped my pain of feeling unattached and used. How was I supposed to tell her, or Justin, that I cried through every breastfeeding and experienced graphic visions while holding Emma Grace? Walking down the steps of our home, I would picture myself accidentally dropping her. Standing over her crib, watching her sleep, I'd have to talk myself into the fact that she was breathing and not just lying there dead.

I loved Emma Grace, but I also felt this horrible, gross resentment toward her.

I wanted her so desperately, but also, and desperately, I wanted my old life back. The one where Justin and I went to the movies or out to eat anytime we pleased. The one where I had at least one visible pack of ab muscles and didn't have to carry around an extra panty in my purse in case of the occasional hard sneeze or laugh. The life where I felt young, unhindered, and had all the energy in the world to run committees, plan projects, and give a care whether my body odor smelled worse than Emma Grace's dirty diaper.

All Rachel had ever dreamed about was being a wife and mother. But all I'd dreamed about was living on my own in New York City, building my own company or landing a lead on Broadway.

Rachel knew me well enough to know that something wasn't

quite right. It was actually her idea that I talk to Ty in the first place. Ty, also from a broken family, could empathize with my experiences. The four of us had talked openly and together about our lives, but never just me and Ty alone. Justin knew about our first phone call, while Rachel listened in. It was shallow at best, a few minutes of encouragement with some "me toos" and "prayin' for ya" thrown in.

A few days later, Ty and I spoke again with permission of the spouses. A few days after that, Justin didn't really seem to notice or care who I was talking to. A few months after that, Ty replaced Rachel as my lifeline.

I talked to her too, but not as much. Ty would call on his break, lunch, anytime he could, to "check on me." Every time I saw his number pop up on caller ID, my heart skipped a beat. Just seeing his name made my palms sweat and butterflies go crazy in my stomach, and forced a huge grin across my face.

Rachel never asked about our conversations, so I never said. Although my heart knew everything about the situation was wrong, my mind was taking a turn for the better.

After months of "counseling" with Ty, I no longer felt sad, scared, or angry. The frightening images of my accidentally hurting Emma Grace had stopped altogether. The days Ty called to check in, I felt like a better wife and mom altogether. I no longer wanted to pull my car off the road and beat the steering wheel while Emma Grace screamed inconsolably from her car seat. The days he called three or four times, I would have the spontaneous and supernatural energy to put on makeup (maybe even deodorant), cook a homemade meal for dinner, and initiate sex with Justin.

Six, eight months passed, and for the first time in years, I had weaned myself off antidepressants. Justin, a man of few words and with little need for affection, seemed thrilled to be free to focus on work. The less time I took for conversation each evening, the more time he had to crunch numbers, visit clients, and make calls. We were making young money, a lot of it.

I justified my conversations with Ty this way: it was a win for all involved.

We still hung out as families—double dates with a shared sitter on Friday nights, lunch after church on Sunday. While the choreography was there, we could all feel we'd lost our rhythm.

It was as if nothing and everything had changed between us.

TAYLOR KNOWS BEST

Ty didn't just ask good questions and laugh at my jokes, he finished my sentences.

He understood what I was feeling before I could put it into words. I could replay pretty much any horrible thought or experience from my past, and Ty had thought or experienced almost the same thing in his past.

He could remember for me too. He remembered what I wore to the Christmas Eve service five years ago. He remembered the differences in my laugh, whether I was faking it for the social elite, self-deprecating for show, caught off guard, or using it to hide something.

While Justin was the best husband a gal could ask for, Ty was the best friend I never knew was possible.

As long as Justin seemed content, our children happy, and my emotional void not so gapping, I wondered if we could live like this forever. I told myself that I was not attracted to Ty "like that." I'd always brushed off his physical features as not my type. But now, after almost a year of finishing one another's sentences, I was questioning whether a girl carrying around the kind of crap I did had any business typecasting.

That first year was thrilling. Taylor Swift's newly released, self-titled album was on repeat in my car and belting out every word of my life. "When we're on the phone and you talk real slow 'cause it's late and your mama don't know." "Drew walks by me, can't he tell that I can't breathe? . . . She'd better hold him tight, give him all her love, look in those beautiful eyes and know she's lucky 'cause . . ."

I raised my hands leading worship at church, prayed openly, taught Bible study to hundreds of women with passion and such ornate, detailed PowerPoint presentations that no one walked out doubting my knowledge of God's Word. During that first year of the affair, I could study the Bible for hours, but Taylor Swift was the one who really seemed to get me.

I believed I could maintain this forever, filled with enough energy to run through a brick wall after brushing against his shoulder while hosting a meal for our young marrieds Sunday school group.

I'd never felt happier and more content in my entire life.

NOTHING TO SEE HERE

We are ever-evolving creatures, changing our minds with little to no warning or explanation. One day we hate broccoli, but then our friend cooks it in a skillet with garlic and oil and it's our new favorite. In one season of life, we'd never dream of questioning our church elders' theological stance, and in another season, we're shocked we ever affirmed it for one minute. *She* would never talk about you behind your back, until she does. *He* would never stay silent while you took the bullet, until he did.

With every birth, death, career move, inspiring sermon, and good book, we change, our minds constantly receiving messages and influencing how we live, both in big and small ways. We are fools not to acknowledge this truth. If we don't, we open our minds to Satan's lie that there is nothing we need to change.

Self-awareness may be the greatest yet most wasted of spiritual gifts.

Self-awareness requires thinking deeply not only about how our past affects our future but also what specifically is changing our minds about our present. Is it a new podcast, a friend's contagious laugh, the way someone parents their child or hosts a party?

Healthy self-awareness is evolving with acknowledgment *and* permission. As our bodies age, so should our minds, with a deeper connection of the *whats* of our past to the *whys* of our present. Acknowledging what specific experience happened to us is the first step. But real growth occurs in the next step: giving ourselves permission to take ownership of that event in real time, putting language on the feelings of the past and receiving feedback from others on how our past presently plays out.

For example, one can feel a brief season of liberation after sharing their story of being bullied in high school. But the maturity that gives that liberty its roots of identity within us is by further welcoming the ideas and opinions from others on how that old wound seems to be replaying itself in our present day.

And because each one of us is able to access our past only from our one-dimensional, subjective worldview, we should be willing to seek out a better self-awareness from the many different voices, experiences, and personalities along the way.

A mature Christian seeks out change.

A mature Christian seeks out change. A person who is truly free in Christ has the self-awareness to learn from others without compromising their own obedience. Seeking out people who are different from us to have our minds changed about something is a wonderful mark of Christian growth.

Satan loves it when we attempt to force everyone and everything into our small, subjective boxes. He wants us to draw hard lines in the sand, believing that this is just the way it is and that I'm right and they're wrong, and becoming so self-reliant that we hate ourselves for needing or asking for help. "All good! Nothing to see here."

The enemy tempts us to believe that nothing around us is changing. Meanwhile, everything is. He doesn't waste his time and energy on humans who are always right, easily satisfied by wimpy worldviews, and quick to surround themselves with people who look just like themselves.

The lie that nothing needs to change within or around us is always the first one we flirt with.

I knew God was there, watching me, warning me like a good parent should, but I'd convinced myself that nothing had changed and that nothing would change, regardless of what I did.

I'd given up on ever being free of the shame and fear that plagued me. I believed that spiritual passion is the same as biblical knowledge, and I made sure not to intimately align myself with anyone older, more experienced, or more discerning than myself.

But then, one regular Sunday morning, right there in the middle of not wanting anything to change, everything did.

TRIGGERED

There we all were, the dream team, doing what we did best: unfolding chairs, arranging the coffee and donut table, one of us praying in a corner and looking over our teaching notes, while the others welcomed our flock of doe-eyed innocents that seemed to be multiplying faster than we could update the email list.

I remember being in midcompliment over a leopard-print

purse that unfolded into a diaper-changing pad when he appeared. Right there in the doorway of the gym, at my church, breathing my air, and now reaching his hand toward the freshly brewed coffee which I had prepared.

Confidently, boldly, with his beautiful wife clutching his arm, there stood Nathan.

My heart started to race, my chest broke out in hives, and my words choked out midsentence.

I'd learned all about triggers in my counseling program, yet I arrogantly always wondered whether they were nothing more than a talking point for people on a never-ending pity-party bender. My excuse for not meeting with a real counselor while spiraling through postpartum depression: "Not a real thing, Kasey. Get over it. Pull yourself up by your . . . on second thought, pull up those deflated balloons you call boobs first. Then we can talk about the boots."

But as soon as I saw Nathan, I was a believer. Everything my professors said was true. Triggers are uncontrollable. They occur when we least expect them and when most everything seems to be fine.

I could not control my internal responses to the external message, the way my body shook and my mind raced. It had been ten years since I'd seen Nathan, yet in that moment it was as if it had happened yesterday.

Frantically I scanned the room, my eyes begging for protection, hope, acknowledgment, pleading for someone to see me and shield me from this intruder. I excused myself to the back of the room, desperate to find Justin. My mind was already drafting his response to Nathan's appearance. "How dare he?! Don't worry, I'll have a talk with him. This will be the first and last time he comes here, honey."

But what I saw next felt like a baseball bat blow to my stomach.

I finally found Justin . . . shaking Nathan's hand and cheerfully welcoming him and his wife into our group.

I couldn't believe what I was seeing. Slowly backing toward the corner, all I could think about was finding the door without drawing attention to myself. In my fury I fought back tears.

I couldn't breathe. How could he shake his hand? Acknowledge his presence even? What twilight realm was I living in? Just then, I felt a warm touch on my left arm. I shuddered and turned sharply. It was Ty. The sight of him just about buckled my knees.

"You okay?" he whispered tenderly. "I'm so sorry."

I wanted to fling my arms around his neck right then and there with no thought for the eighty oblivious people yacking around me. It didn't matter that no one else noticed me. Ty's face, knowing me and seeing me like this, made me feel like the only one in the room.

> God doesn't waste the wounds we've buried. He orchestrates events to resurface them for healing.

CHAPTER 15

Sift It Out Now, Sinner

I DON'T REALLY KNOW WHAT I EXPECTED JUSTIN TO DO WHEN he met my rapist face to face. Inside, I wanted him to be every man I'd always wanted all at once. I wanted him to be the father I'd never had, holding me tight and whispering, "Honey, hand me my shotgun. No man's going to touch my princess like that and walk away with his manhood." I wanted him to be my protector and get quickly to work on an elaborate operation to exact my revenge. I wanted him to be the romantic, pouring me another glass of wine while I blubbered. "Just let it all out, honey. He's a jerk and we hate him. You just go right on and cry while I put on some Justin Timberlake and rub your feet. Tea tree or lavender?"

I wanted him to save me.

But instead, Justin woke up the next morning like he always did, put on another button-up shirt, kissed me goodbye, and whistled his way out the door to work.

Justin knew of Nathan and what he had done to me. He could recognize him in a crowd, but neither of us had ever run the scenario of his family showing up at our church. Nathan had become everything people said he would become: business savvy, public servant, community leader. I'd run into his wife from time to time, secretly peering at her from behind the sleeve of a shirt I was admiring at the department store.

I assumed Nathan had never mentioned me to her. And nothing about her presence ever seemed to evoke more than a lump in my throat. She was attractive, no surprise there.

By the time Nathan's family showed up in town, I no longer needed to concern myself with his whereabouts or the unacknowledged trauma he'd caused in my life. Because I had Ty. And Ty finished my sentences.

Oh, Justin was still as kind and gracious as ever, maybe even more so. The weight of responsibility for providing for our massive mortgage and growing family seemed to fuel him. He may have been cussing me under his breath at the office, but he never let me see even an ounce of dismay over my frequent Pottery Barn purchases. He wanted me to make our house a home, and for the kids to have the best smocked gowns and handstitched leather boots.

Still, I couldn't remember the last time we'd sat, just the two of us, over a bowl of chips and salsa and talked for hours. For that matter, I couldn't remember the last time I'd taken my shirt off to have sex. I was embarrassed by the milk-crusted deflatables now drooping to my belly button. I mourned my perky youthful self who'd felt confident and classy in her V-neck T-shirt. And I mourned the butterflies that once fluttered about in my stomach over a simple come-hither look from my very own Wrangler model.

Justin's Wranglers had been replaced with starched khaki slacks, and the euphoria of our sex life came in a strong second to the excitement of watching a new episode of *The Office*.

I've heard most people struggling in their marriage say something like, "It feels like we are just roommates instead of husband and wife." Yet the opposite felt true of me and Justin. As far as we were concerned, we were crushing it in marriage. We never argued or disagreed. Our home and finances were in pristine order, and our kids behaved in public. Every Christmas card was styled with the perfect mix of pattern and solid jewel-tone, and every elaborately-themed birthday-party invite (including monogrammed return-address label) was delivered within the four-to-six-weeks timeframe good etiquette required. Sex was not often but consistent enough and all I'd ever known it to be. Sex had only ever complicated things for me, so not being asked to entertain it daily, even weekly, made Justin even more endearing.

DEEP FRIED HAPPINESS

By the time we'd made it through the catfish lunch buffet after my second day of Nathan, I'd already given up on Justin. He didn't know it, because I was proficient in faking it. To his credit, he had not been completely aloof, apologizing if "shaking Nathan's hand and welcoming him to our group had resurfaced old wounds." And while it's always so heartwarming when someone apologizes *for* you (not), the real salt in the wound came with his next sentence. "Maybe he's changed. I didn't know what else to do. What did you *want* me to do?"

I paused. Looked straight into his eyes like he was the dumbest person on the planet and said, "Would you even understand if I told you?"

His face dropped. I'd wounded him. But in true cowboy fashion, he'd rather sit quietly and wait out the storm than work himself into a tizzy trying to find a way out of it.

It was years before Justin asked me another important question. Unbeknownst to the both of us, there would soon come a time when he would be forced to make a little noise and fight for what he wanted, but for now, we silently agreed that we were very different people than the ones who longingly said "I do."

As he broke my gaze to cut up a piece of his fish for the baby and I looked down at my phone to see if Ty had had a chance to slip away for a check-in text, it was obvious we were both now content with just a side hug.

In the small country diner down the road from our home that we frequented so often the owner kept our family Christmas picture pinned behind her cash register, I made a choice.

As I paid our bill at the register, and with Justin's gubernatorial voice muddled in the background at our table like the voice of Charlie Brown's teacher, I stared at the picture of my perfect little, put-together family behind the counter. For the first time in a long time, I thought about my mom and dad when they were still married. I wondered about the day they also made this choice. Shockingly, I empathized with them, felt sorry for them even. How long had they fought? How misunderstood had they felt? How many months passed between sexual advances or passionate kisses? Had it been years since they'd thrilled at one another's touch or felt seen by each other in a room full of people?

As I let out one long sigh and snapped back to reality long enough to plaster a friendly smile on my face—"Thank you, ma'am! Enjoyed it as always. Tell that sweet man of yours I said hey!"—I felt the anger and resentment I'd harbored for so long toward my parents lift right there along with the aroma of fried pickles and corn muffins.

No, I didn't want a divorce.

But I did want to stop waiting for happiness.

That day, I chose to be happy on my terms. My way.

I'd fulfill my duties as a wife, mother, daughter, and Sunday school leader. But I would also stop waiting on God and stop depending on Justin to pull me out of this funk. "How could I be so weak," I thought, "letting Nathan make me a victim all over again?" I was stronger and smarter enough not to let one glimpse of him send me spiraling all over again. And Justin—well, I never should have trusted him with my happiness in the first place.

SMALL-MINDED DELIGHTS

God loves us more than our happiness. He offers more than happiness too.

As it was with my marriage, the core problem with our unhealthy choices, our culture, and so many of our American church houses is not the fact that we have feelings but instead that we need to feel all of the time.

God, using our feelings to communicate with us, has no desire for us to detach from them. But he does want to fulfill them as only he can.

God wants to satisfy our longing souls and to fill our hungry souls with good things (Ps. 107:9). He promises to give us the desires of our hearts when we—can you finish the sentence? Is it "trust him," "obey him," "repent of our sinful ways," "give of ourselves more," or "go to church more frequently"?

The text reads, "Delight yourself in the LORD, and he will give you the desires of your heart" (Ps. 37:4 ESV). When we delight in him, we also receive the desires of our hearts.

Such a powerful and profound word chosen by God. He could have said any of the other options. He could have said nothing at all. But he chose to connect what we most want with what we most enjoy. He created our feelings and affections to be direct lines to our identities, so it breaks his heart that we are so easily pleased with the small-minded feelings marketed to us over media, and the simplistic affections of men and women.

Why have only happiness when we can also have joy? Why just be still when we can "be still, and know" (Ps. 46:10)? Why enjoy just one fruit of the Spirit when God wants us to enjoy all of the fruit all at once? "But the fruit of the Spirit is love, joy, peace, patience, kindness, goodness, faithfulness, gentleness, self-control; against such things there is no law" (Gal. 5:22–23 ESV).

When we delight in God, our hearts will naturally overflow with desires calibrated to his will. When we enjoy him, find pleasure and ecstasy in him, we will want what he wants, know what he knows, grieve what he grieves, and feel what he feels. When we delight in God, our feelings can roam and play freely because they are gauges, not guides.

Satisfied feelings allow us to hang out with people who act, believe, and engage life differently than we do without our being swayed or swallowed up by them. The more we delight in God, the more we can exist in high stress, volatile, or intense environments without taking negative energy into ourselves. The longer we delight in God, the more frequently we do or feel things for the benefit of others instead of for our own benefit.

> **When God has deeply satisfied our feelings, it is our joy to deny them.**

When God has deeply satisfied our feelings, it is our joy to deny them.

Yes, I had a rough upbringing. I was a victim in every sense of the word. I was also an offender, no better than Nathan, Cory's neighbor, or a guy spending his next forty years in prison.

But mainly I was an overzealous Christian girl searching so desperately for her significance that she was unwilling to deny herself anything.

I loved God, but I still had a duty to self.

I didn't want to accept the infringements upon my innocence or let the guilty go unpunished. I didn't want to confront how easy it was for me to abandon intimacy, or take ownership of how easily others had abandoned me. I wanted to feel happy, loved, appreciated, and as if my life matters to this world in some way. I wanted the perfect marriage, home, and children. I wanted to drive onto the road of life whenever I felt like it, however I wanted to, and with no one commanding me otherwise.

I only thought I hated my unattached and broken heart when in reality I loved it.

I had fallen in love with my hurt because it could justify my feelings.

I had worked my entire life, using all of my resources, to craft the image I wanted everyone to see. In doing so, I'd denied myself nothing.

If I wanted to resent someone, I did. If I wanted to be angry and bitter, I was. If I wanted the rush that comes from adultery, I took the hit. If I felt like casting someone out of my life because they made it more difficult, I was like, "Bye, Felicia!" If I wanted to feel better about myself the next day, I went to church.

So what was the most loving thing God could have done for a Christian gal like me, bent on uninhibited desire?

Stand back, give her some room, and let that little girl drive her Barbie Jeep straight off a cliff.

BOOM-CRASH-SLAP

You know what I love most about the Bible? It's full of sinners, regular people like you and me.

Early on in my Christian life, I thought the people in the Bible were placed there to be our role models, examples of how we are to live if we really want to honor God. I would happily bebop along for a few chapters of Noah's radical obedience, Moses' humble longsuffering, and David's bold faithfulness, until *boom-crash-slap.*

Why had my Sunday school teachers left out the whole "naked-drunk, impatient-insecure, cheating-murderer" parts of their stories?

I'd feel confused, caught off guard, and a bit betrayed watching them fall from atop the mountain of spiritual zeal. I wondered, "If *these* guys can't get it right, then how the heck will I? Should I just skip over these parts? Pretend I didn't just read about Moses' missing out on the one moment he'd sacrificed his entire life for? And don't even get me started on King David. I swear, you give a guy a little time on his hands in view of a naked girl just minding her own business and it's never going to turn out well."

How am I supposed to model myself after all of these boneheads?

The good news is, I'm not supposed to. Neither are you—oh, please don't. Learn from them? Yes. Admire them? For sure. Keep telling their stories to our children and their children? Absolutely! Why? Because they are us and we are them, the story of humanity connecting to one another and the God who saves us all from ourselves. The story of their lives is written for no other purpose than to point out the glorious goodness of the Author.

Whether it's Old Testament "hall of faith-ers" or New Testament Christians, no one is steadfast toward God. We have faithful days and unfaithful days. Even our most obedient, spiritual moments fail compared with the perfection God requires for entry to his presence. So God wrote an entire book about people who need saving just as much as we do.

> God wrote an entire book about people who need saving just as much as we do.

We watch their stories like good movies, drifting in and out of sinful seasons, up and down the rollercoaster of betrayal, suffering, victimization, and victory.

None of them ever arrives. Not one of their stories plays out the way they'd planned. Just when one of them starts to think they've got God all figured out, *boom-crash-slap!* Another twist and turn crashes into their stories. And not because these God-fearing men and women have no legitimate feelings or desires to serve God but because they are not yet willing to deny their feelings or desires in service to him.

America makes it easy to forget that Christianity places little priority on one's comfort. And it certainly does not promote spending hours considering how better to incorporate "self-care" into one's daily routine. The call of Christ is not easy. And if you can't remember the last time you've really sacrificed, truly given up a want or need for the sake of someone else, then you might want to prepare yourself for your own *boom-clap-slap.*

God loves you like he loves Noah, Moses, David, and the whole motley crew. He loves us enough to slap that selfishness right on out of us.

Or, as in Peter's case, to sift it out.

WHEN YOU HAVE

"Simon, Simon, behold, Satan demanded to have you, that he might sift you like wheat, but I have prayed for you that your faith may not fail. And when you have turned again, strengthen your brothers" (Luke 22:31–32 ESV).

Our day of sifting may come just as it did for Peter: while we're standing eyeball to eyeball with Jesus.

Peter, one of the most beloved disciples and the founder of the Christian church, most likely felt unbreakable and unstoppable after the high he'd been on experiencing Jesus' miracles and teachings firsthand. Knowing that Peter gave up his home, family, job, and reputation to follow Jesus leaves little doubt that Peter believed *in* Jesus. And yet one questions whether Peter had ever truly denied himself long enough to actually *believe* Jesus.

This much is true, God never sifts any of us unless we've given him reason enough to.

> **God never sifts any of us unless we've given him reason to.**

Peter would not deny himself, but he would deny his friendship with Jesus before realizing how much it meant to him.

The same is true of us.

If we do not believe that God is worth our delight, we will waste our lives chasing every desire other than the one that's able to fulfill us.

Peter was just your average fisherman when Jesus called to him and his brother, Andrew, from the bank of the sea. Based on what we know of his occupation and hometown, Peter may have cussed, drank too much, treated himself once or twice to a visit to the "red light district." At the very least, he could have held his own with the crude, uneducated men who had little choice but to inherit their father's trade. He kept odd hours, fishing at night instead of the day. And if fish was all he had for wages, he was most assuredly from the poor side of the tracks.

He wasn't the man you and I would have chosen to set as the bedrock of the church (Matt. 16:18), but he was God's perfect man for the job.

Think of what it would take to be a professional fisherman. Peter must have been patient yet determined, a man strong enough to haul in heavy, waterlogged nets yet gentle enough to hold and clean those wriggly fishes. He was most likely a self-starter, focused, with the negotiation skills to sell his fish to market, able to forecast the weather, and just desperate enough for something in his life to change that he would leave all of it behind once the opportunity presented itself.

Jesus didn't need just any man to help him change the world, he needed a Peter. Everything about Peter's past would have been relevant to God's calling on his life. No part of him would have been wasted, not his personality, passion, or choices.

Because God had every intention of using Peter's whole life, every divided and fragmented piece of him would have to be sifted through until Peter was made whole, until all of his feelings, thoughts, and behaviors became one with God's will.

Even in the warning to Peter that Satan had received God's permission to mess with him, Jesus still assures Peter that he will come out on the other side.

"And when you have turned again." Not if you turn but when you turn.

Before the foundation of the earth, God chose Peter to fulfill this specific purpose. God knew it, but Peter didn't. So God proved it to him.

Anything that Peter might use to hold back from claiming his rightful place in God's promise simply must resurface. Not for God's sake but for Peter's.

As God did for Peter, so he does for you and me when there is even an inkling that we're tempted not to trust him. In love, that we may see and know our whole stories, the real story, God hands us over to Satan for the destruction of our flesh (1 Corinthians 5).

And as with Peter, my sifting was not pretty. As you know, it led me into the darkest night of my soul, a day no one dreams of as a little girl or wishes on her worst enemy.

The rebellion of adultery resurfaced every tired self-preservation pattern of my youth, like self-harm and substance abuse. The extreme rush of adrenaline needed to maintain such a secret required payment in increased blood pressure, insomnia, chronic headaches, and the buildup of stress-induced toxins in my bloodstream.

Over the course of two years, my sifting led to handfuls of anxiety attacks and two hospitalizations. My sifting dropped me from 140 to 98 pounds, caused the hair to fall out of my head, ushered in my first cavities, made eczema break out on my arms, and aided in the formation of a malignant tumor in my abdomen.

Like Eve, I had been deceived, and my mind led astray from a "sincere and pure devotion to Christ" (2 Cor. 11:3). My conduct was overtaken with sin (Gal. 6:1). I had turned against my very own body (1 Cor. 6:18), and now I was at war, not with other people or myself but against the rulers and authorities "over this present darkness" (Eph. 6:12 ESV). My divided, depleted, detached self could hardly lift herself out of bed each morning, much less wield a sword "against the spiritual forces of evil in the heavenly places" (v. 12).

If it were just about my sin, or yours, we would be crushed under the weight of it. Think about all of the ways we distrust God every day, all of the things we say and don't say, give and withhold in a matter of moments or hours. It's too much. Sometimes, I don't even realize I'm sinning. Some days, my habits are just so deeply engrained that I cannot see the damage they've done until something important has crashed and burned at my feet.

> Our sin is the only thing strong enough to kill its own self off.

In God's eyes, the course we take in our lives is not just about our sin. There's no sliding scale or big and little sins at the foot of the cross. Instead, the purpose of God's permitting our sin is to produce the destruction of it. Our sin is the only thing strong enough to kill its own self off. We wouldn't know that our delights were so weak if we never tested them out.

Humans rarely see wickedness and rebellion the way God does—as useful.

I know it seems the most unlikely tool God would use to speak to us, but that's because, well, we're American.

We can hardly stand for our toddler to explore five feet away from us without rushing in to save him or dousing her with antibiotic. We can lose our minds when unsaved people continually act like they need saving, and freak out when the saved ones struggle to believe they really are. We're a bunch of fixers, meddlers, and debaters, lighting up around the same fire.

We don't want bad things to happen to good people. But few of us are turning our cell phones off long enough to admit that not a one of us is good, and that just maybe, God is using the bad in our lives to slap, sift, and sober us all up to that reality.

So God permits us to wander off long enough to take away our appetite for straying.

And as with Satan, the end of our sin is inevitable.

As Christians, we belong to God, and he will not allow any one of his children to sin successfully. It may take months for our distrust to run its course. It may take years. For those who have struggled long and hard in abuse, neglect, poverty, or illness, it makes sense that survival, not surrender, has become a way of life and that it may require a little extra time for us to break through.

What about you, oh sinner? Have you been, are you being, sifted?

Not sure how to answer that? That's okay. I get it. Really.

So here's a better question. The most important.

Do you hate your sin?

You see, a person without the Holy Spirit has no guilt or shame over their desire to distrust God. They rarely consider what degree of risk they pose to themselves or others with their choices. Oh, sure, they may sit next to you in church, but that doesn't mean they also feel remorse over the big and small ways they are distrusting God. There is only one way to be certain of our salvation, one test that we will indeed go to heaven when we die.

Do we hate our sin?

I'm not asking if you want to sin, because some big or tiny part of us may still want to. I'm not asking if you enjoy your sin, because that's a no-brainer. We all enjoy the indulgences of the flesh. Plus, we are all fully capable of doing something we enjoy while hating ourselves for it.

I'm not even asking if you feel bad about your sin. Most people feel bad about lying, cheating, stealing paper from the office. One can have a guilty conscience and still go to hell when they die.

I'm asking, specifically, do you hate your sin? As in, when you contemplate sinning or choosing to sin, it grieves you. You feel disdain and strong dislike to the point of pain at the mere thought of distrusting God with this choice. And not because you've failed some moral obligation to humanity but because you've turned against your true self.

God is using our lives to show us a faith that no longer turns on a dime, a relationship with him that no longer caves to emotion or rushes into the arms of another. So he gives us over to our sin that we may finally be done with it.

Like Peter, myself, and countless others, your sifting may come when you least expect it, or when you're standing face to face with Jesus. But if you truly hate disbelieving who God says you are, if you really want to believe him, I implore you to let the sifting happen. Let your sin be about the business of killing itself off, taking with it every wimpy, unsatisfied desire until not one of them is left standing.

No matter how many years you've been shaking your fist, shopping, or sleeping around, once God's sights are locked in on you, it's only a matter of time.

Weep, mourn, sing, shout, and dance if you hate the thing you also want to do. For you are really saved and really going to heaven. Only authentic believers feel sorry for their sin. So if you do, go right ahead and drop to the ground, scissor-kicking through the loudest belly laugh you've got. Because you're in. He wants you.

You are not too far gone, too sinful, or too boring.

But you *are* his.

> God does not waste our sinfulness. He uses it to establish himself as the more desirable option.

CHAPTER 16

I Don't Know How to
Not Love You

"I'm going to talk to Ty," Justin casually announced into the bathroom mirror as I straightened my hair.

"You're what?!" I snapped, wide-eyed and dumbfounded, two seconds away from burning three inches off the end of my hair.

"I've already called to let him know that I'm about to head that way. I told him that he doesn't need to worry or get upset. I just want to talk. That we can sit out on the back porch or something away from the kids."

"Justin. I . . . this . . . why . . . what are you going to say to him?"

I felt like I was in the thinking corner of my kindergarten music classroom, bending over to discipline one of my unruly five-year-old students. "Now, Cade, your decisions affect more than just you. See all of your friends here? Tell me, how were you thinking about them when you made this choice?" Something about Justin's inexperience with transgression, his innocence in dealing with the darker side of things, motivated the mama bear in me to step forward to protect all involved.

I questioned whether Justin had fully grasped that he, too, had lost a best friend.

While he had never depended on Ty to the extent I had on Rachel, his trust had been doubly broken. Regardless of how it all went to crap, all four of us were grieving the loss of not just whimsically fun nights out on the town with a couple that "sure seemed nice," not just a seasonally perfect match for our kids and our marriages, and not just friendship, but the loss of our family, a way of life, the only life we'd known since the first month of our marriages.

And our hometown was much too small to keep going in any one direction of our lives without derailing our entire way of life.

In the few months since our secret hit the fan, Justin and I had been asked to quietly remove ourselves from every leadership role we held in community or church. Without a word, I was removed from every email list, planning committee, and Facebook group in which I held office or rank or gave once-welcomed guidance.

Every baby or wedding shower, women's brunch, and vacation Bible school that I was scheduled to host or participate in sent a short but sweet email or handwritten letter excusing me from service. Well, except for the campus Baptist Student Ministry. I'll give the directors credit. They at least had the courage to retract my invitation to share during student lunch with a face-to-face explanation. "Please understand, in light of recent events, we feel you are just not the best person to be sharing with our students. It would open the door to too much speculation and unnecessary questioning."

My gut reaction was that my earliest assessment of the BSM's weekly hamburger lunches had just been confirmed. But I was in no position to be having gut reactions to anything. Although I secretly believed that in light of recent events, I was the *best* person to be sharing with their students, they were right about the timing. Not ideal.

I had no business leading or running anything at this juncture, but the whole "without a word" thing made me feel disgusted with myself, and I was determined never to lead anything ever again.

I think that's why small-town sin is so much stickier than where it's easy to blend in with the masses. In a small town, most people think they know you. Which also means that when you mess up, they also think they know how to fix you. But perhaps the small towns of the world do get one thing right: there's a church on every corner. Got to take care of all those up-close and personal sinners whose dogs won't stop pooping in your yard.

Still, I felt worse for Justin, Rachel, and our kids. They hadn't asked for any of this. They shouldn't have been forced to pay the price of a sin they didn't commit. But in a small town, you are guilty by association. And as long as they stood by us, they would go down with us.

Justin could no longer work out at the gym without someone staring at him. His coworkers seemed to treat him more nicely than normal. Emma Grace often came home crying after preschool because she and her best friend from birth, could no longer play in the same group at school.

My pastor's daughter, Cory, always said that I would break Justin's heart. She said it while standing in front of my pastor. He chuckled. One of those "joking, but not really" moments. I was pretty sure I knew what he was thinking now. I pictured him sitting over his heaping plate of fried catfish just down the road from our house: "Mmm-hmm. Saw that one coming." Or maybe, even worse, he hadn't thought about us at all. We wouldn't know if he had. We hadn't been to church in two months, and during that time, we heard not a word from anyone there. No check-in offering to pray with us or help us through.

The silence was the hardest part. Because we knew people weren't really silent. We knew they thought something, said something—just not to us. We were at the mercy of everyone else's version of the truth. And nothing about that felt forward-moving or healing. Just dark, narrow, and painful.

We had no idea how interlaced our lives had actually been with Ty and Rachel's until the relationship lay broken on the ground in front of us. How had we been so naive? Why had we turned a deaf ear to the warning sirens, a blind eye to the red flags that always fly highest where God's altar is replaced by mortal idols?

Our way of life with Ty and Rachel was all we'd known of adulthood. It would be impossible to start a new way of life. We drove the same streets, shared the same church, school, and friends. We served on the same committees, ate at the same restaurants, shopped at the same grocery store, and filled up at the same gas station. I still had bags of Rachel's shoes in my closet that I'd borrowed for a trip. Ty had tools in his garage that belonged to Justin. Our kids were scheduled to walk down the aisle holding hands as the ring bearer and flower girl next month at one of our best friends' weddings.

I couldn't drive anywhere without coming face to face with one of them. There was no side street, vacant lot, or empty park that didn't remind me of stolen moments.

I had waited eight weeks with still no word from Rachel. I dreaded and desperately craved the opportunity to apologize to her face to face. It's all I had talked about since Justin's worst day.

"*That's* why I'm going, Kasey. Maybe once Rachel knows I've forgiven Ty, she will forgive you too."

Silence. Tears welled in my eyes as Justin turned toward me, leaning his cute butt on the vanity, his voice deep, solemn, and, for the first time since I'd know him, almost a whisper.

"If Ty is going through anything close to the hell you've been through, and if there's a chance I can help him, if there's even a chance he is waiting on my forgiveness, then I just have to tell him. I can't say I've forgiven you and not forgive him too."

You're absolutely right, reader. My heart melted like butter right then and there.

As I pulled his nearby hand into mine, whether or not he wanted me to, I could only hope the tiny, one-winged shudder of my stomach butterfly was mutually felt.

The charm of the moment did not last as the reality of the situation fluttered more frantically inside my head. My mind raced as I replayed my confession. Had I told Justin everything? Did anything more need to be said?

Confession had played out differently for me than it had for Ty. He'd most likely been living through eight weeks of intense female interrogation. I, on the other hand, had gotten off easy. Not only did I have a compartmentalizing, logical, no-details-please male to answer to, I had a cowboy. If the situation didn't call for a pushing, prodding, or roping, then someone was just overreacting.

Regardless of whether I'd rambled it out before, I had to make at least one thing clear before Justin met with Ty.

"Justin, I know I have a bad track record with relationships. And I know I need to work through so much stuff buried deep inside here," I said, pointing to my heart. "But I need you to hear me be honest right now. Because if I don't say this now, I may never say it. And because . . . as much as I hope you don't, you may want to leave me after you hear this. Which, I totally understand if you do, but please don't take the kids, I beg you, please . . . I never meant—"

"Kasey," he interrupted.

"Sorry. Okay, I'm just going to say it then. After all of this, I don't know if I even know what real love is. But as far as I do know, I was and still am in love with Ty."

For just a second, I squeezed my eyes shut and braced like I might get slapped. I quickly readjusted. "But!" I said, opening my eyes, looking straight into his, grabbing his other hand, "I also love *you!* I love you *so* much! I didn't know it was possible to . . . you know, love two men like this? I don't know . . . but you are good to me, to the kids. You are everything I . . ." Tears forced me to stop talking.

Justin let me cry for a few minutes before he said his next words, the ones he'd most certainly been rolling over in that not-so-simple cowboy heart of his during the past two months that had laid waste to our home.

"Kasey. I may not know exactly what love is either. I thought I did. But now. I don't know? If I'd really been loving you, I don't think any of this would have happened. That's what feels so strange about all of this. I hate it. I mean, it makes me sick and sad. I don't really want to see Ty or . . . be around you." He hung his head to break my gaze.

"But. If none of this had ever happened, I don't think I would ever really know what love feels like. How painful and messy it is. How much it can hurt you, and still . . . well, here's what I do know." He stood straight up, dropping my hands to reposition himself, and was now towering over me and looking down into my eyes.

"I don't know how to not love you."

And yes, reader. I melted all over again.

SCRAPPY, MESSY LOVE

Our words were scrappy and all over the place. None of it may have sounded eloquent to someone listening in, yet it was a perfectly tuned symphony to the ears of our hearts. It would go down in our story as the day we were both finally set free to know real love. Not all at once or right away, but soon enough. And more quickly than our small town would ever give God credit for.

Ty barely said a word to Justin the entire thirty minutes they were together. Because, no surprise, Ty could hardly speak past the lump in his throat.

Justin repeated to Ty exactly what he'd rehearsed with me.

"Ty, I've forgiven Kasey. And if I've forgiven her, then I also forgive you. But, Ty, hear me say this. Our families will not be in one another's lives from now on. I don't know how this will look day in and day out in this town. We need to be patient with one another as we all do what's best for our marriages and kids. But," he said, turning his face directly toward Ty, who sat at his side staring at a nearby creek, "you will *not* contact my wife again."

Ty sorrowfully nodded his head and attempted to speak.

"Justin, I'm just so . . . *so* sorry. I don't even . . ."

Justin was surprised by the tears now welling up in his own eyes at the sight of this big, burly, broken man who hadn't shaved in weeks. His recent memory of his wife's own brokenness, spewed out onto the floor, had softened Justin to the full measure of forgiving and loving his Judas.

Justin held up his hand for Ty to stop talking. He had little left for words after our earlier conversation. "I accept your apology, Ty. It's done. Now, go love your wife and your kids. Because that's what I plan to do."

As true forgiveness always does, the moment hoped to duplicate itself. Not long after Justin's meeting with Ty, I literally bumped into Rachel at our shared grocery store. After several seconds of embarrassing pleading on my part, she hesitantly agreed to talk to me.

She chose a playground we'd often frequented with the kids, in the middle of the day when there was sure to be plenty of spectators. Not my ideal spot for asking forgiveness for deceit and adultery, but as we've established, I held a crap hand.

Whatever made her most comfortable was best. And I would just have to deal.

I can sincerely say that I've never been more nervous about a situation in my entire life. I've never been anxious enough to make myself sick or to tremble into a cold sweat. But I was that day.

Every warning in my spirit was telling me not to meet with her. Seems contrary to what God would want, right? Delay forgiveness? You know, the "do not let the sun go down on your anger" rationale (Eph. 4:26 ESV). Unfortunately, the sun had risen and set many times before this moment. Rachel's anger had formed deep roots of bitterness. She wasn't angry, she was cold. I knew it the moment I rounded the corner of the pasta aisle and crashed my cart into hers. I felt defeated before I ever said a word as she glared at me with an ice-cold, blank expression.

Once at the park, I also started crying before I ever said a word, so that didn't help matters.

Watching Emma Grace rush into her son's arms, reuniting with shrieks of excitement and possibility, just about undid every ounce of fortitude I'd mustered to show up in the first place. All of it made my knees want to buckle. But not Rachel. There she stood, stoically pushing her daughter in the swing while I awkwardly forced Lake's supersized fat rolls through the leg holes in the swing next to hers. I started pushing. And all I heard for the next five minutes was the sound of her breathing through the noise of the squeaky chain.

The whole thing went as badly as you want to imagine.

Before I could make out the words, she rapid-fired back to me, "I forgive you," as layers of muscles tensed below her cheekbones.

I knew she didn't mean it. But there was little I could do or say in the presence of other mothers and toddlers to convince her that *I* really was sorry.

It was a good thing too, because every minute that passed of her silent seething was another minute I seemed to forget why I wanted to apologize.

It was an impossible tension for us both. All we'd ever known was the dance of friendship. A gritty, safe place to air our honest feelings with one another. I kept fighting the desire to just reach out and hug her. And she, despite how cold she was, seemed grieved by the fact that I no longer could.

After it was obvious nothing more could be said, we gathered the kids, fake-smiled over them as they said their goodbyes, and walked one behind the other toward the parking lot, as we had so many times before. Car seats snapped closed, *Veggie Tales* cheerfully sang through the closed suburban doors, and then . . .

"Sorry, what was that?" I hollered over the top of my Yukon, balancing on the edge of the open driver's door. Rachel was saying something from her rolled-down window on the other side. I stepped down and around, "Sorry," I said the word one more time for good measure, "I couldn't hear you. What was that?"

And there it was. What she really thought of me.

We threw word grenades at one another for the next ten minutes.

I know, I know. You're thinking, or should be anyway, how did I have the audacity to speak one word of rebuttal to her? Because I'm a jerk. Really. Anytime I am not synced up to the Holy Spirit, I am only and always thinking about myself, not what is rational, kind, generous, or helpful.

The more she talked, the more heated I got. Arrogantly leaning against my passenger side door, I couldn't believe I was hearing all of these words after what my husband had said to hers.

Old-school Kasey creeped to the surface. And old-school Kasey is scrappy. If you see me take off my earrings, run. Because I'm about to lose all my Jesus on you.

Plus, old habits die hard. All I'd ever done my whole life is fight instead of feel. The more insecure, wrong, or disgusted with myself I was, the harder I fought to prove I wasn't any of those things. It made sense Rachel would tap into her scrappy side too. She felt insecure, ticked off, betrayed beyond measure, jealous maybe?

That day, between the two of us, a bomb of female emotions went off in a preschool park, with twenty innocent-bystander moms as witness. Bless them, they'd left their own houses that day to get away from the shrapnel of hormones.

SMOKE AND FIRE

Traumatic experiences are not always bad. Most of the time when we hear the word trauma, we associate it with something bad. But the official definition describes it as any event when our emotions cannot catch up to our reality fast enough, an experience that feels so far outside of our awareness, we have no memory of how to deal with it other than our basic, animal-like survival skills.

If you think about it this way, we've all been traumatized to some extent. Yes, some more devastatingly than others, with longer lasting effects, but all of us have found ourselves standing in a situation thinking, "Is this really happening right now?"

> Trauma overwhelms what has been true long enough for us to realize it no longer can be true.

Trauma overwhelms what has been true long enough for us to realize it no longer can be true.

That's what Justin's words did to me—they traumatized me.

His forgiveness of my unthinkable sin brought me so high and so low all at once that my whole life went into a tailspin, drastically and forever changed.

Justin admits that his words to me moved through him like a supernatural force, not motivated by any one feeling and certainly not attached to his affection for me but instead as an out-of-body and one-with-God experience, denying his desire to lash out and leave, while delighting in a God who'd also forgiven his worst days.

"I don't know how to not love you."

Spoken as if Justin's whole life was meant for this very moment. The words to our very own love song—excuse us, Taylor.

It would take someone as naive and innocent as Justin to conceive such a response. Much like it would take a baby, innocent, pure, untainted by wickedness, to offer himself in such intimate form to a world and to hearts as broken and as cold as our own.

My entire life had also been building up to this very moment, the moment I finally stopped running from my life and instead embraced it. The moment I no longer simply believed *in* God as my Savior but *believed* him as Lord. The moment my past was no mere random collection of events but an intricately designed masterpiece of plan and purpose.

God's love traumatized me, shifting my reality and closing the gap between what I'd thought was true and what was.

Justin's words were not his own but God's Spirit breaking through the cold, bitter, hardened places of my heart and shaking me, sobering me up to my reality.

For it was God who did not know how to not love me.

He had always loved me, chosen and designed me to be loved by him.

No matter how far away I thought I'd run, he was always there.

No matter how bad and disgusting my sin, God used it to sift and sanctify the real me to come out of hiding.

No matter how broken a promise felt, God had kept the only one that mattered.

"Neither death nor life, nor angels nor rulers, nor things present nor things to come, nor powers, nor height nor depth, nor anything else in all creation, will be able to separate us from the love of God in Christ Jesus our Lord" (Rom. 8:38–39 ESV).

How would I ever have known his precious promises without a reason to believe them?

The degree to which we doubt our position is the degree to which we disbelieve God's promise. Why wouldn't he traumatize us to get our attention?

Your trauma may come in the form of a first kiss or a devastating heartbreak. It may come through marriage or divorce, a new birth or a painful death. God may draw you back to himself through a whisper in a vacant, back-alley lot or through a booming voice inside a packed church.

> **The degree to which we doubt our position is the degree to which we disbelieve God's promise.**

Forgiveness, sincere grace to let someone off your hook of need, will always be the match that lights the fire of authentic faith. God's grace is the only love in control enough to look at our worst motives and still forgive us. No man or woman is designed to walk the road of unconditional love with us to the end. That's a job only for the source of love himself. But we can walk longer stretches with others the stronger our spiritual muscles become.

And this is really all we are looking for in people, right? It's true as a counselor, a parent, an employer, a friend. We are looking for, hoping for, longer periods of time between unhealthy choices. That's it!

When I'm working in therapy with an addict, I don't expect them never to want to drink again. In the first few months, even the first year, I'm not surprised if they relapse. All I am charting in the way of growth in healthiness is longer stretches of time between the harmful choices to drink. Three weeks between drinks, then three months, then three years. Now that's maturity!

Growth doesn't change the fact that they were once an addict and probably always will crave alcohol to some extent. Moving forward in no way diminishes the long, hard road it has taken to get here or the broken relationships left in our wake. Instead, maturity acknowledges that we are all still on the same road we've always been on, but now we are able to stay upright for longer periods of time.

This is the strength I've found in owning my story and sharing it with others.

It's the hope that Justin and I found to take another step, then another, until one day, we looked behind us and couldn't believe how far we'd been able to walk.

Rachel and I didn't end that day at the park whole and healed. For many years after, I prayed for her, begging God to let me receive her real forgiveness once and for all. Some nights, it was all I could do not to pick up the phone and call her until she caved or to show up at her house on my knees begging for mercy.

That day at the park, I responded to her in my flesh, not in the Spirit, because grace was still a new language to me. Although I had been a Christian most of my life, and one who often preached grace to others, I had never received grace for myself. I could quote Scripture all day long, but I had never been awash in those Scriptures as though they were true of me.

God's words through Justin had begun a new thing in my heart, but I needed some practice. I'd never walked the steps of faith as a free person, believing that God wanted me and chose to love me. And judging by my epically failed apology to Rachel, there was still loads more work to be done. But I'd been traumatized by a God who could never not love me. Once my emotions caught up to his reality, I would never be the same.

With my thirties fast approaching, I knew that whatever came next, I was stronger and more likely to trust God. With my family still intact, albeit by a thread of grace, I felt like I could walk forever, determined to enjoy and delight in God more than I ever had before.

Perhaps his love becomes real to you at age seven, thirty-seven, or eighty-seven, inside a prison cell or inside the prison of your tormented thought life. However and whenever God makes himself real to you, trust the smoke, fire, and rubble of a life shattered at your feet. For it is here, in your weakest, most vulnerable state, in the unlikeliest of places, that you will hear his voice most clearly.

When he reaches for your mouth with a hot, burning coal of conviction, embrace your pain, own your sin, and delight in the grace you've been given to simultaneously cry, "Woe is me!" and, "Here I am! Send me."

> And the foundations of the thresholds shook at the voice of him who called, and the house was filled with smoke. And I said: "Woe is me! For I am lost; for I am a man of unclean lips, and I dwell in the midst of a people of unclean lips; for my eyes have seen the King, the LORD of hosts!"
>
> Then one of the seraphim flew to me, having in his hand a burning coal that he had taken with tongs from the altar. And he touched my mouth and said: "Behold, this has touched your lips; your guilt is taken away, and your sin atoned for."
>
> And I heard the voice of the Lord saying, "Whom shall I send, and who will go for us?" Then I said, "Here I am! Send me."
>
> —ISAIAH 6:4–8 ESV

God does not waste our traumas. He uses them to overwhelm us into grace.

CHAPTER 17

Living Like It's Our Job

FORGIVENESS IS BOTH THE CATALYST FOR AND EQUALIZER OF the unwasted life. Forgiveness is a terribly wonderful reality for all of us. Terrible, because it requires us to absorb any debt we've held against another. Wonderful, because we hadn't realized just how heavy all of those debts had become.

Many people say that forgiveness is based not on feeling but on choice. But I think it's both-and. I believe our overwhelmed, exhausted, extreme feelings are to blame for finally pushing us over the cliff, leaving us little choice but to forgive or spend the rest of our lives miserable.

Once we grant forgiveness to another, it will take time for our new, healthy feelings about that person or experience to catch up with our choice.

Like the old-school Kasey resurfacing in the park with Rachel, old wounds and triggers remind us that we need to commit to the daily practice of denying what may come naturally to us and instead doing something different.

This means an alcoholic should stop buying beer, someone living in debt should stop going to Target "for groceries." If you're in love with pornography, cancel your data plan. If you hope for better friendships, start being the friend you want, and if you claim to love Jesus more than anything, then love him more than anything.

Reading the Bible is the most practical way to help our feelings catch up with the truth of who we are in Christ.

Not long after "I don't know how to not love you," I put myself on a strict and daily Bible-reading regimen. Now, before you roll your eyes thinking you're in for another episode of *Stuff Christians Say*, I want you to know that I've read the Bible almost daily since I was a teenager. I read it all through my promiscuous teen and young adult years. I memorized it, taught it, and sincerely have always been one who geeks out on Hebrew and Greek commentaries and hermeneutical textbooks.

But as I learned post-repentance, reading the Bible as already true of you instead of as waiting on you gives it a whole new meaning.

> Reading the Bible as already true of you instead of as waiting on you gives it a whole new meaning.

God's Word takes on new context and meaning through the lens of grace.

If we approach the Bible wrongly believing that God needs something from us, then reading his words will feel heavy, cumbersome, and overwhelming. But approaching the Bible as though God needs nothing from us opens us up to enjoy him, chewing on each verse as a rich, tasty morsel that goes down into our core as satisfying and delicious.

Reading the Bible is the absolute first step to, well, everything, because God's Word is the only story capable of changing our hearts. While human stories can change our minds, they are not strong enough to change why we do what we do. "For the word of God is living and active, sharper than any two-edged sword, piercing to the division of soul and of spirit, of joints and of marrow, and discerning the thoughts and intentions of the heart" (Heb. 4:12 ESV).

If we want anything in our lives to change significantly, reading our Bibles is the choice we must make every day, no excuses. We may not feel like reading or have a clue what we are reading, but the more we practice, the more God will open our spiritual eyes to see people and experiences the way he does.

Voices with microphones tend to change their truth with shifts in the socioeconomic climate. But God doesn't need a microphone, podcast, bestselling book, seat in an office, or sold-out arena to speak absolute truth to us. His Word is never changing. And contrary to popular belief, his Old Testament nature is never compromised by New Testament grace.

My encouragement to anyone who is leery of approaching their Bible is this: pick it up and read. Start wherever you start, and read until you get out of your head long enough to hear him. Read until your spirit speaks to you. Read until his opinion becomes more important than yours.

FROM THE INSIDE OUT

Grace always flows from the inside out. Our God-honoring actions will never truly honor God if he does not hold the place of honor in our hearts. This is why forgiveness is the key that opens the door to freedom in the Christian's life. The more truly forgiven by God we feel, the more desperate we will be to release others from paying us back for their wrongs against us.

This is always the flow of obedience: from the inside out.

Obedience does not beget forgiveness. Forgiveness begets obedience.

We all reach a point in our stories when something must shift to reach the resolution. As I hope you've seen in my story, a Christian can walk an awful long time in the same circle, rearranging their behaviors enough to fool themselves and others without any real transformation.

Not until a force stronger than our desires and more complex than any subjective truth smashes into us will we be traumatized enough by grace to believe who we are in Christ.

Forgiveness is this trauma.

Forgiveness is the decision to let another person off the hook of our need. It's the painful choice to look at our offender or attacker, that mean girl, our betrayer, parents, or friend in the face of our deepest wounds and say, "I release you. I release you from apology, acknowledgment, remorse, or payback for the way you have wronged me."

Forgiveness like this has no quick-release trigger. It often begins with the simple awareness that something is weighing us down. That something looks different for all of us. Maybe you want to be free of paralyzing fear surrounding a dream you've always hoped to pursue. Perhaps you want to be free of nagging guilt or shame over past choices. I think it's safe to say we all want to be free of insecurity and the traps of comparison.

Your need to forgive someone could be as vague as a nagging feeling in your gut or as layered as an unresolved parking-lot throwdown between wife and mistress that occurred years ago. Perhaps it feels like a daily choice to look past an offensive personality at work or the rebellious choices of your children.

Regardless of what has led you to this moment, choosing to absorb one another's debts (all at once, over the course of years, or all day every day) is the joy that enables us to face anything without sinking or crumbling. Our reserves of forgiveness overflow from the assurance that God has also forgiven us. And this gift traumatizes us with the reality that everything really can be forgiven.

Everything. Like, the worst of the worst.

"As the Lord has forgiven you, so you also must forgive" (Col. 3:13 ESV).

Not until we receive God's grace and forgiveness for ourselves are we able to give grace and forgiveness to anyone else.

My entire life has played out exactly as it was designed to—expertly orchestrated to help me receive the forgiveness that had always been mine in the first place.

Yours too!

Do you see it?

We need God's grace first. Otherwise, we'll spend the rest of our lives turning on ourselves and each other.

> Not until we receive God's grace and forgiveness for ourselves are we able to give grace and forgiveness to others.

Oh sure, we may find happiness for a time. We may be healed for a season. We may be at peace for a moment. But without claiming the gift of God's unconditional love for us, we will never be whole.

This is the gospel, the good news that God's love will always interrupt the most intimate places of our hearts to share in a whole relationship with us. In the Old Testament, God's presence dwelled inside the most holy place of the tabernacle, accessible only to the high priest, who made sacrifices to atone for the people.

But when Jesus died, "the curtain of the temple was torn in two from top to bottom" (Matt. 27:51) as he became the once and for all sacrifice. Now, our bodies are temples of the Holy Spirit within us (1 Cor. 6:19) and Jesus, the Son of God, is our great high priest! Because he enters *through* relationship, *for* relationship, we have the confidence to draw near to him in order to receive mercy and find grace to help us in our time of need (Heb. 4:14–16).

God sent himself that we might be integrated with who he is and what he is doing not just here and now but forevermore.

God doesn't want us to be just healed, just redeemed, just saved, obedient, faithful. He wants us to be whole. He wants our motives to match our thoughts to match our behaviors, over and over again, until our confidence is so strong in him that we, "being rooted and grounded in love, may have strength to comprehend with all the saints what is the breadth and length and height and depth, and to know the love of Christ that surpasses knowledge, that you may be filled with all the fullness of God" (Eph. 3:17–19 ESV).

COMING HOME

During the past ten years of professional counseling and Bible teaching that has taken me all over the country, I get one question more than any other: "How do you know God's will for your life?"

My first answer, as you might guess, is, "If you're not reading your Bible every day, you haven't got a chance." The quick second to this is, "You won't find God's will behind the doors you're trying to beat down."

Remember, God doesn't *need* us, he *wants* us.

He doesn't need us to run things, dream dreams, make a lot of money, or pursue fantastic careers. Although we may do all of those things, we might also have to clean houses to pay the rent on 750 square feet for the rest of our lives.

> We won't find God's will behind the doors we are trying to beat down.

Above all, God wants us to trust him. Anything we feel the need to make happen is most likely not from God. He doesn't want us to force our way into things, but instead he wants us to wait for him to bring things into our lives. This means we can trust the organic. If you didn't have to elbow someone in the face to get there, then go ahead and walk on through. You may epically fail once you do, but that's okay!

Because we are responsible not for the result, only the faithfulness it takes to get there.

We are called to obey God, nothing more, nothing less.

Every morning when we wake up, our only job is to obey God in everything—the words we say, the places we go, the groceries we buy, the tattoos we get (okay, that one's for me). But seriously, I have to ask the Lord if I can get my next tattoo. If I need to tap into my family's savings account in order to do so, it's not an option. If the image I want to ink is going to remind me of painful, secret things, then no. If I'm still living under my parents' roof and a tattoo would really tick them off, not helpful. If the artist has no openings, not the time. All of it matters.

A few years ago, I wanted my next tattoo so badly. I could have chosen not to pay one of our medical bills that month and had enough money to do it. But then I would have been guilty of making it happen. Against my desire, I waited. After a few weeks, I got a call from my brother, who was on his way to get one and asked if I'd join him for moral support. While we were there, the artist next to him happened to be available, and my brother secretly paid for it when I wasn't looking.

I know that seems trivial, but not to God.

He loves my tattoos! As long as I am obedient to him in the process, that's all that matters.

When we received the phone call asking whether our family would be willing to move to a new town for a new job, not for one second did we question whether it was God's will, although every second leading up to it terrified us.

The call came from a contact we'd made more than ten years ago as newlyweds. I'd been accepted to a seminary program in another town. Although not one realtor called us back in the course of six weeks, Justin put in his resume with the town's insurance office, just in case.

We gave up on my seminary dream after every door to it seemed to close, and instead, we decided to build our own dream right where we were—in our hometown.

The subsequent years of our investment in our hometown is what made the idea of moving so ridiculous.

For starters, we'd built a massive home. And not just any home, our dream home. We'd spent two years designing it from every magazine clipping I'd saved through college.

Also, we'd situated our dream home across the road from another important home, Justin's parents'. The Van Norman compound planted itself on three hundred rolling acres of the most picturesque ranchland Texas has to offer, fully stocked with cows, horses, dogs, cats, you name it. The plan was for Emma Grace and Lake to grow up in our pineywoods castle, learning to handle animals and ride at a young age, and for our home to one day become the cool hangout for all their teenage friends on Friday nights. And we loved the free babysitting and home-cooked dinners at the grandparents' every week.

Then there was Justin's job. Justin had become a reputable insurance agent in our hometown, growing his book of business from five to six figures. He'd worked hard to build his client base. In the insurance business, you can't take your clients with you when you leave. It's unheard of to make a lateral move in this industry, because doing so forces you to start from square one.

When we got the call offering Justin a small book of business two and a half hours down the road, none of the logistics made sense.

Mostly what motivated us to move was the fallout from the affair. Lack of church home, loss of friends, people who'd known us forever now shunning us. Emails and letters telling me how awful I was. Silence from our family members, because, awkward. Backroom meetings with our church elders lasting well into the night, going round and round about how best to deal with both our families attempting to coexist in the same congregation.

Deep in our bones, Justin and I both knew, despite what seemed rational, that East Texas was no longer our home. The fallout from the affair had uprooted us from this place. Every day after, it had been like trying to walk through mud. Nothing about our lives was natural. It was as if we continually needed to remind ourselves and everyone else that we belonged here.

So as Justin spent our last week banging his head against the wall while turning over the fruit of a decade's worth of work to his replacement, I spent my days packing up a house that was once a dream and now a nightmare. How had I ever justified the size of my shoe closet alone with so much of the world's population still dying of hunger?

Feeling out of our minds, we loaded up a twenty-foot cattle trailer, hauled 25 percent of what we owned to College Station, Texas, and moved ourselves, a toddler, and a kindergartner into a cramped, low-income neighborhood in the middle of town. Our rental was approximately 750-square feet, and I cleaned houses for the next year to help pay rent.

We'd moved to the college capital of our state, where Texas A&M University was home to a whopping sixty thousand students. Our house shook with every touchdown. (As in the rumble of field artillery canons and fly-over jets.) But after years of waking up to horses trotting against the backdrop of sunrise and birds chirping and a crisp breeze smelling of pine and hay, we were not prepared to spend Sunday mornings walking our fenceline picking up the littered beer cans and cigarette butts from the after parties in our neighborhood.

We'd gone from organic to food stamps, Pottery Barn to Wal-Mart, and a flexible budget to a color-coded three-by-five-foot whiteboard mounted on our mantle with line items on it. Most of our family could hardly find the strength to speak to us, and the kids screamed all night every night that they wanted to go home.

It was awful. And magical.

The first day I went grocery shopping, I felt like Martha Stewart prefelony. It had been so long since I'd leisurely browsed bath rugs or taken the time to smell melons for ripeness. I couldn't remember when I'd last pushed my shopping cart with my eyes looking up and forward, not down to the floor. Without fear of bumping into any who thought they knew me, I felt free to enjoy life's simplest pleasures, like discovering that Starbucks sold their coffee on grocery store shelves now and unapologetically shoving a bag of grounds into the stranger standing next to me: "Did you *know* about this?!"

Our first Sunday visiting a new church, the greeters at the door welcomed our family like royalty. They kept shaking our hands and hugging us as though they'd just found us after searching for us for days. They kept handing us free things, like pens, journals, stickers, tissue, a new key chain. All precious and welcome things to a newly broke family.

We sat through the entire church service without one stare drilling a hole in our backs and without wanting to pass notes to one another about where we'd go afterward for lunch.

Yes, all new things feel dazzling when you first open them. But for the Van Norman crew, our new town felt like the only thing we'd never known was missing from our lives. Home.

Not one day since our move has it felt like anything different.

God never wastes the gaps. He fills them.

CHAPTER 18

Big-Picture Believing

A Home for Unlikely, Improbable, and Discarded Things

"KASEY, STOP RIGHT THERE, OKAY?!"

Justin took large steps toward me with both hands in the air motioning for me to stop walking.

It was dark, about 9:30 p.m., and I was exhausted after a long day entertaining a passenger vanful of teenagers at the public swimming pool. All I wanted to do was unlatch my bra, not *even* brush my teeth, and fall into bed.

The gravel crunched louder beneath his feet as his form appeared more clearly through the darkness. I stopped walking when I saw the expression on his face. He looked as if he'd seen a ghost. My heart rate went up, because Justin never panicks about anything.

One time, a car T-boned me and a friend while we were riding her Harley through our neighborhood. We were fine, with the exception of my left foot, which jammed into the motor, breaking three of my toes. When we returned, Justin looked at my mangled foot, which had already doubled in size and was horribly bruised, and said calmly, "Huh. Weeellllll, I've got some Tylenol at home?" He was one-hundred percent serious. It took me ten minutes to convince him to take me to the emergency room.

I started to panic because Justin and I were now the full-time, care-custodians of eight teenage girls who had every reason to snap at any minute. If Justin was telling me to "stop right there," it was likely because he was preparing me to calmly receive news that my dinner plates were now smashed or that "so and so" had run away again.

Within the first three months of working on the staff of a children's rescue ranch, I'd had one knife pulled on me, one fist-sized hole in my living room wall, several broken windows, one sex sneak-out, two sex sneak-ins, and many detailed commentaries on where I could stick things.

But now we were seasoned. After two years of living onsite as a staff family, little shocked us. We'd learned to roll with the ever-changing climate not only of nonprofit work but also of caring for traumatized, wounded children who were desperate for someone, anyone, to love them.

Most of the girls we cared for were victims of sex trafficking and abusive relationships, all of them neglected, abandoned, and exposed to the worst this world has to offer. Their choices were juvenile detention, the street, their pimps' sofas, and us. Students arrived via the police department, a concerned relative, or the FBI.

Most of the girls in our home had been with us for more than a year and felt like daughters. We did homework together at night, made lunches for school, laughed, fought, went shopping. They played dolls with Emma Grace or pushed Lake on his training wheels in the front yard. Typically, if we could convince them to stay through the three-month honeymoon phase, they were more likely to graduate and receive a donor-given scholarship to college.

Just when we started to catch a good rhythm in our house, a new admission would shift the energy just enough to trigger an avalanche of insecurities and survival behaviors. Our day at the pool had been my and Justin's best effort to distract them all long enough to remember fond childhood memories.

Our chatty bunch of "not tired yet" beauties had been sent to the showers while I returned the van to the staff lot and Justin put Emma Grace and Lake to bed.

Walking toward our home through the main road of our ranch, Justin moved cautiously toward me.

"What's wrong?!" I picked up the pace.

"Nothing. I mean, the girls are okay. Just, listen for a second."

I shifted back on my heel, stretched my hand to my hip, and rolled my eyes. Justin was by far the pushover of the group. "What did they do?" I said solemnly and suspiciously.

"No. It's . . . it's not the girls or the kids." His words trembled with—fear? Excitement? I couldn't tell. I'd never seen him fidget and fumble for words like this. I stood up straight and furrowed my brow for him to hurry up and spit it out.

"It's. It's *Rachel*," he blurted.

My mind couldn't compute what he was saying. I thought he was trying to tell me a new girl was on the way or that I had been saying someone's name wrong all this time. I was confused.

"What are you talking about, Justin? Who's Rachel?"

"*Rachel*, Rachel! She is sitting in her car in our driveway *right now!* She wants to talk to you!" Justin was completely freaking out, more panicked over a situation than I'd ever seen him before.

I pushed past him and started to run. I didn't really know why I was in such a hurry to get to her. A vision of her punching me in the face or pulling out a gun flashed through my mind. I quickly scanned for the girls. Still showering, thank God. As I rounded the corner to our driveway, I couldn't help but let out a small snicker. No surprise, Rachel and I had the exact same car, same color and model. They were parked side by side.

It had been five years since the last time our cars were parked side by side. Five whole years since I'd seen or heard anything involving Ty and Rachel. And here she was, unannounced, unexplainable, parked in front of our singlewide staff trailer. Here I was looking as ragged and worn as ever—damp T-shirt, shorts, squeaky Tevas, flat pool hair, no makeup.

As I approached her driver's side door, I could hardly believe I wasn't shaking or scared. Or questioning Justin's eyesight. But as the door unlatched, I saw that Rachel's petite figure, ever-classic hair, and porcelain skin had not changed a bit. Seeing her standing across from me sent a wave of the strangest and most shocking feeling. I felt as if, somehow, we were still friends. I was almost excited to see her and fully expected her to come inside and sip coffee and talk loudly while I blow-dried my hair, like we used to. An awkward, misplaced smile spread across my face as her eyes met mine. I knew she was taken aback, because she took a step backward.

"Too much," I thought. "Just chill."

"Rachel?" I said warmly. "What are you doing—"

She cut me off midquestion. "I'm sorry to just show up like this. A friend told me you worked here now, so I googled the address." Her voice was shaking, yet controlled.

"You drove all this way?" I said. "Please! Come in!" I took a step toward our front door, but she stayed frozen where she was. Justin slowly took a seat on our front porch steps, on the periphery, doing his best not to draw attention to himself, yet desperate to be included in this conversation.

"No. I mean, no thank you." She paused. "I only need a minute of your time." She looked down at her hands, rolling her ring around her finger as she tried to find her words.

"Okay." I planted myself, being sure not to cross my arms over my chest.

"Kasey, I want to say two things. First, I forgive you. I mean, I forgave you a long time ago, really. But the Lord told me I needed to tell you to your face. So when I heard him tell me to get in the car and drive here today, I was scared and it's crazy, but I just did it."

My eyes filled with tears and it took every ounce of strength to keep my heart from bursting out of my chest.

"Second. I want to ask your forgiveness."

My chin dropped.

"We all had a part to play in this, and I didn't handle things right or well. I'm sorry for the way I treated you, Justin," she glanced over to him, "after everything . . ." Her voiced trailed away.

I didn't know what to say. It felt completely absurd for *me* to offer acceptance to *her*. After all this time, I hardly knew what she was apologizing for. I could barely see Ty's face in my mind if I tried. Seeing Rachel again did resurface old feelings and memories, but not as they once were.

Where once was shame now lived confidence. Where once I desired big waves of lust and passion, now I desired simple pleasures and adventures, like thrilling at my husband's touch, a van full of rowdy, misplaced souls, and running alongside my son as he peddled his bike by himself for the first time. My greatest regrets had turned to gratitude, and my most painful seasons of loss to the reason I was born.

"Please come in, Rachel. Really, I . . . I don't know what to say."

"Do you forgive me?" she prompted.

Hesitantly, almost embarrassingly, I replied, "Yes, of course I do! And you have no idea what it does for me to hear you say that you forgive me! I've prayed for years—" My tears choked me short.

"I know," she said softly. "I'm sorry I didn't tell you sooner."

Seconds of silence passed while we shuffled our feet. Her mission was complete, and I knew she would turn to leave at any minute. So without a thought to my words and actions, and reaching from the most natural, pure place in my heart, I raised my arms, humbly looked into her eyes, and said, "It's okay if you can't. It doesn't change a thing. But before you go, may I have a hug?"

Neither one of us scored high on the physical-touch scale of love languages, so I knew this seemed completely out of character. Yet I couldn't help but sense that both of us needed to touch one another, to physically display to all the shuddering demons who may have been watching that Satan did not win this one.

She politely nodded and leaned in for my embrace. It lasted only a few seconds, but they were the most enlightened seconds of my entire life, the whole picture of it a bold spit in the face of every time we are tempted to disbelieve that our lives are unfolding exactly the way they're destined to. A fist in the gut of all the lies we tell ourselves about things being too broken, too far gone, irreparable.

Our hug was real and sincere. An audacious declaration of a God who seeks to redeem and reconcile not just the easy but also the hard, complex, and complicated. A testament to the tension, intimacy, and vulnerability required to experience the full-circle offering of a holy God to his unholy people. A proclamation to no longer be satisfied in our one-way lanes of salvation, healing, or living well but instead take God up on his offer, demanding that our lives be lived as the whole people we were made to be.

The circle our arms made around one another set off fireworks inside my heart and mind. In that moment, I felt sure that no part of my story had been wasted.

Nothing about my past was meant to be dismissed or downplayed. It was meant to shape me, define me, and prepare me to receive this moment. This unlikely moment, with the most unlikely of people, in the most unlikely of places.

I could have held onto her much longer, but with tears in her eyes, Rachel squeezed my shoulder, nodded her goodbye, and drove away. As her taillights melted into the night, I watched for as long as I could. Justin's hand reached around my waist and drew me to him.

Without a word, we both released a long, audible sigh of

glorious release. As we did, the sound of teenage-girl chatter broke the silence. Arms wrapped tightly around one another, we marched in sync to meet up with our girls, likely to throw out onto the dinner table whatever cereal boxes we could find while they tormented one another over who would get the last pink tube of Great Lash mascara.

All of them, in some way, were me. All of them, in some way, needed a man like Justin.

Who ever would have thought that the pair of us would spend the rest of our days making a home in "the land of misfit toys," turning over our story a hundred times a day for the sake of broken, discarded pieces of humanity?

God, that's who.

It may have taken us thirty years to accept his offer to use the parts of us we thought we'd lost forever. But once we did, we never stopped thanking him for the ways *no* part of us ever was lost, just in process.

FOREVER SURE

When Jesus comes into our lives, he gives us a promise that forever changes us. This promise is ours to use daily in big and small ways, in difficult or easy seasons of life.

His promise is that no part of us is wasted.

We see it, perhaps, most clearly here, in his Word:

For those whom he foreknew he also predestined to be conformed to the image of his Son, in order that he might be the firstborn among many brothers. And those whom he predestined he also called, and those whom he called he also justified, and those whom he justified he also glorified. What then shall

211

we say to these things? If God is for us, who can be against us? He who did not spare his own Son but gave him up for us all, how will he not also with him graciously give us all things? Who shall bring any charge against God's elect? It is God who justifies. Who is to condemn? Christ Jesus is the one who died—more than that, who was raised—who is at the right hand of God, who indeed is interceding for us. Who shall separate us from the love of Christ? Shall tribulation, or distress, or persecution, or famine, or nakedness, or danger, or sword? As it is written,

> "For your sake we are being killed all the day long;
> we are regarded as sheep to be slaughtered."

No, in all these things we are more than conquerors through him who loved us. For I am sure that neither death nor life, nor angels nor rulers, nor things present nor things to come, nor powers, nor height nor depth, nor anything else in all creation, will be able to separate us from the love of God in Christ Jesus our Lord.

—ROMANS 8:29–39 ESV

There is an assurance offered to us in Jesus, revealed to us throughout our lives. And that assurance is the certainty that God loves us just as much now as he always has, and that he always will. No matter how bad it gets on the outside or inside of us, he still loves us. There is not one thing you have done, are doing, or will do that can bring you back into condemnation. Why? Because the debt has been paid! Finally and fully.

And God doesn't pay debt like humans pay debt, with IOU slips still floating around out there in the no-man's-land of our brains. Unlike humans, God does not expect us to pay him back.

Instead, he pays our debt completely, as only a holy, perfect, sacrificial love can: by absorbing it.

God didn't just place our sin and suffering "over there" or "over here" on the periphery of our lives. He took it onto himself, absorbed it through the pores of his skin into his own blood, and in doing so, he carried it to hell, where it belongs.

No other religion in the world but Christianity serves a God who died and rose from the grave in human skin. Through Jesus' res-

> God loves us just as much now as he always has, and he always will.

urrection, God is asking us also to uproot what we once thought dead and let it give new life to others. His life welcomes us to take all of the broken, discarded, darkened parts of our stories and use those pieces to show others what true love is.

Resting in the assurance that my own debt is paid was the only way I could forgive Nathan without ever receiving a word of acknowledgment or apology from him. God's love was the only force strong enough to help me reclaim sexual intimacy with my husband and entrust my children to God when they veer dangerously close to repeating my generational sin. God's grace was the only grace deep enough to reconcile me with my father, Rachel, and the long list of people lying in the wake of my past.

God is offering you the confidence that *all* things truly work out for our good and for his glory (Gen. 50:20, Rom. 8:28, Isa. 43:6–7).

DOMINO

Test me on this if you don't believe me. Set up the dominos of your past and watch them fall one by one into your present.

Here, I'll show you mine.

Because my parents were divorced, I was drawn to the acceptance of a small youth group in a conservative Baptist church in East Texas, where I learned the foundation of my faith and where I received my first Bible. Because my mom asked me to move out of our house, I moved in with the Bennetts, who also hosted the annual college costume party in their garage.

Because my drama teacher paired me to dance with Nathan, I was just sassy and mad enough to show up to that costume party ready to break all innocent cowboy bystanders who might be present. And because the roads were too iced over for Justin and me to go anywhere else on our first date, we were forced to sit for hours asking each other important questions.

Because Justin was born to his parents, and I to mine, we married into one another's differences, sometimes filling, other times creating the gaps within ourselves. Because Justin's confident nature pulled up folding chairs for a new young couple in our Sunday school class, we learned the joy to be found in community and friendship. Because I was insecure and unattached, needy love came easier for me. Because Justin was secure and attached, not needing love came easiest for him.

Because Ty was so exhausted with our sin, he forgot to delete our phone records, leading Rachel to find them, exposing our adultery. And because I had once attempted to pursue seminary, Justin made an insurance contact that called him ten years later, offering him a job in another town with a do-over we never knew we wanted.

Because we moved to this new town, I received an emergency hysterectomy by one of only ten surgeons in the country who was able to robotically perform the procedure, which naturally shifted my female organs out of the way to reveal a golf-ball-sized malignant tumor in my abdomen.

Because all of my friends were new and untied to my past offenses, they were able to fully give themselves to my family, caring for us throughout the two years of my chemotherapy treatments and into my remission. Because cancer changes everything and forces one to live to the fullest, Justin and I walked onto a child-rescue ranch, hoping just to volunteer. Instead, we walked out with jobs. We were offered these jobs because one of the directors happened to read my first book, while the other director had recently posted a position for a trained equestrian instructor and licensed counselor.

Because we worked for a public-record place of business, Rachel was able to find our address. And because she did, Justin and I now step out each day, our heads held high, assured that no part of us has been wasted. Even better, every part has been purposed for loving and serving others.

Now our family runs a small farm offering employment and care to women and children in need of a fresh start. Droves of college students from our town's crazy-big campus now frequent our back yard as volunteers, cleanup crews, and tutors for the children we serve.

Justin and I get unbelievable invitations to travel, together sharing our story of restoration with others who think their stories are the most unlikely, improbable places to start. Some weekends, the crowds are big and fill an arena, but mostly, they are up-close and personal relationships in our everyday lives: a man in another state who is desperate for the strength to forgive his wife and with whom Justin prays over the phone from the rocking chair on our back porch each Sunday night. A woman without a penny to her name doing what she has to in order to get by, playing dominos with me around our kitchen table.

These are the faces and stories of our unwasted lives. Regular people, feeling their way to God through the unlikely twists and turns of their stories, all of us interconnected.

Look into your past, reader. Let the spinning plates of your secret shame, hidden agenda, or exhausted lie come crashing to the floor so that they may finally be used for what they were purposed: to serve.

Coming full circle with our past does not put an end to our

pain but instead gives us eyes to see its purpose and, more important, to see the pain of others.

> Coming full circle with our past does not put an end to our pain but instead gives us eyes to see its purpose and, more important, to see the pain of others.

Taking God up on his offer to be exactly who he's always been means that we no longer need to force our love into places or require it from others but instead can live holy and whole right where we are, present and purposed.

Once Justin and I did the hard work of reconciling our lives to God, we were set free to love as pure children who trust and obey their Father not because we have to but because we want to.

THE END. YOUR BEGINNING

Tag, you're it!

Do you have a history of abuse or neglect? Go find someone who also has been abused or neglected.

Do you know the pain of losing someone close to you, the agony of rejection, the fear of human comparison? Then sit with someone long enough to say, "Me too!"

Are you a victim? Then love another victim to their victory.

Are you an offender? Then show up unannounced and unexpected to beg your victim's forgiveness.

Do you struggle with depression, anxiety, materialism, or addiction? Then lift your gaze to a world of people who are hurting, helping, and hoping right alongside you.

And what about this Jesus? Do you love him most? Has he traumatized you with his grace? Do you rest in the assurance that he will never leave you or forsake you?

Reader, if he's knocking at your back door right now, no matter how unexpected or chaotic life feels, please don't hesitate. Open the door and let him in.

He is not here to condemn you. He is here to enjoy a relationship with you. He doesn't need you, he wants you, simply because he's never known how not to love you.

So when you acknowledge before others that he's been standing there all along, he will also acknowledge you before his Father in heaven (Matt. 10:32).

When he walks through your door, you might be tempted, for one moment, to think it was you who turned the knob. Until you behold the words on his outstretched hands: "You did not choose me, but I chose you and appointed you that you should go and bear fruit and that your fruit should abide, so that whatever you ask the Father in my name, he may give it to you" (John 15:16 ESV).

If you've been gracious enough to abide with me this far, reader, it is highly probable that Jesus has been after you this whole time, pursuing you over the course of your life to be transformed by the greatest love of your life, the hero of your story.

Justin could have walked out on me, but he stayed.

Jesus could have left us to destroy ourselves, but he stayed.

And if Jesus did not abandon us when hell itself rained down on his shoulders, why in the world would we think he's going to give up on us because of a few rough years or bad days?

If God did not spare his own Son for his glory, he will not spare one moment of our lives for that same glory.

Oh, dear reader. How I pray this end is only your beginning.

Thanks for letting me go first.

> Nothing is wasted. Not even this moment right here.

Notes

1. Citations for my research for chapter 5: Inge Bretherton, "The Origins of Attachment Theory: John Bowlby and Mary Ainsworth," *Developmental Psychology* 28 (1992): 759–75; R. Karen, *Becoming Attached: First Relationships and How They Shape Our Capacity to Love* (Oxford, England: Oxford University Press, 1994); John Bowlby, *Attachment and Loss*, vol. 1, *Attachment* (New York: Basic Books, 1969); Mary D. S. Ainsworth, "Attachments across the Life Span," *Bulletin of the New York Academy of Medicine* 61 (1985): 792–812; John Bowlby, *Attachment and Loss*, vol. 2, *Separation: Anxiety and Anger* (New York: Basic Books, 1973), 246.

2. C. M. Leaf, *Switch On Your Brain: The Key to Peak Happiness, Thinking, and Health* (Grand Rapids: Baker, 2013); The American Society of Human Genetics, "Six Things Everyone Should Know about Genetics" (July 26, 2010); Ingrid Lobo, "Environmental Influences on Gene Expression," *Nature Education*, 2008 (accessed July 27, 2010); Kristen Philipkoski, "How to Turn On a Gene," *Wired*, February 6, 2002 (accessed July 27, 2010).

3. Gerhard Kittel, Gerhard Friedrich, and Geoffrey W. Bromiley, *Theological Dictionary of the New Testament* (Grand Rapids: Eerdmans, 1964) digital edition.

New Video Study for Your Church or Small Group

If you've enjoyed this book, now you can go deeper with the companion video Bible study!

In this six-session study, Kasey Van Norman helps you apply the principles in *Nothing Wasted* to your life. The study guide includes video notes, group discussion questions, and personal study and reflection materials for in-between sessions.

Study Guide
9780310104209

DVD
9780310104469

Available now at your favorite bookstore, or streaming video on StudyGateway.com.